Grammar Girl *Presents* *the* **Ultimate** **Writing Guide** *for* **Students**

Grammar Girl *Presents* the **Ultimate** Writing Guide *for* **Students**

Mignon Fogarty

illustrations by
Erwin Haya

St. Martin's Griffin
NEW YORK

www.stmartins.com

Designed by April Ward

Grammar Girl™ and Quick and Dirty Tips™ are trademarks of Mignon Fogarty, Inc.

The Library of Congress has cataloged the Henry Holt edition as follows:

Fogarty, Mignon.
Grammar Girl presents the ultimate writing guide for students / Mignon Fogarty ;
with illustrations by Erwin Haya.—1st ed.
p.   cm.
Includes bibliographical references and index.
1. English language—Grammar.   2. English language—Rhetoric.
3. Report writing.   I. Haya, Erwin, ill.   II. Title.
PE1112.F6127 2010   428.2—dc22   2010011699

ISBN 978-0-8050-8943-1 (hardcover)
ISBN 978-0-8050-8944-8 (trade paperback)

Originally published by Henry Holt and Company

10 9 8 7 6 5 4 3 2

For my niece Mya,
and for all the kids like her who
are just starting to love writing

USING THIS BOOK

Many sections in this book have been numbered so we can easily refer you to them from other parts of the book. The first number refers to the chapter and the second number refers to the section. For example, section 3-16 refers to Chapter Three, section 16.

Contents

Grammar Schmammar

THINK A GRAMMAR book has to be annoying, boring, and confusing?

Think again.

I'm Grammar Girl. I correct errors for a living. I even have a podcast about grammar. (Check me out on iTunes.) Writing is hard enough without being overwhelmed by nonstop rules, so that's why I'm here—to make those dos and don'ts understandable.

Let's face it: everyone writes. Sometimes writing is the only way you communicate with someone. Between creative writing, papers, and reports in school, it never stops, right? Add status updates, text messages, and blogs, and your life is a writing fest!

Why care about writing? Good writing allows you to express what's in your head so that others can understand. What's the point of having a great idea or an amazing story if your writing messes it up?

I think of grammar as rules for the game of writing. Knowing these rules will give you the confidence to produce the best writing you can and make sure your ideas are taken seriously.

Sure, English is full of conflicting rules, similar-sounding words, and exceptions; but I'm all about making complex explanations fun and easy to understand.

What I'm not trying to do is make you sound like everyone else or like you're from Shakespeare's time. I'm here to give you Quick and Dirty Tips: tools, crazy memory tricks, funny phrases, and grammar cartoons of Aardvark (an aardvark) and Squiggly (a snail), all so that your writing will reflect you, your thoughts, your research, and your ideas.

You'll even get tips to jump-start your writing, help you with revisions, and make sure your school papers don't get those dreaded comments: "redundant," "awkward," and "confusing." We'll also talk about what's appropriate for all your writing: e-mail, letters, text messages, and school papers. Finally, we've created a website with quizzes and exercises to reinforce what you've learned. Visit grammargirlstudent.com.

Aardvark

Squiggly

If by the end of this book you find yourself addicted to grammar, to the many wonders of the comma, or to spotting apostrophe misuse, don't fight it. Embrace your inner grammar guru.

Chapter One

Parts of Speech

IN **THESE NEXT** few chapters, think of me as your grammar guide, intent on demystifying grammar. I'm a practical person— I've given people batteries and socks as birthday presents. That is what I want to give you, the things everyone will use—the batteries and socks of writing.

In order to do that, we need a common language between the professionals and us. If I quickly spewed out terms like *antecedents*, *future progressive tense*, and *subjunctive verbs*, you'd probably run away screaming, but you do need to know some of these terms and what they mean. I promise to explain these words (and their usefulness) and, if I can, give you other words to use in their place.

To begin, you need to know the parts of speech, the function of different groups of words. In Chapter Two, you'll use this knowledge to put together sentences. After that, punctuation. Then the world is your oyster.

Or your pizza.

I prefer pizza.

NOUNS

A **noun** is a person, place, or thing. Things can be concrete, like rocks, or abstract ideas, like courage or purpose. Nouns are divided into two types: proper nouns and common nouns.

Proper nouns name *specific* people, places, or things, such as *Grammar Girl*, *Mississippi River*, and *Golden Gate Bridge*. They are names. On the other hand, common nouns name *general* people, places, or things. The words *girl*, *river*, and *bridge* aren't capitalized because they are common nouns that don't name any one individual person, place, or thing.

QUICK AND DIRTY TIP

If you don't know whether to capitalize a noun, see if it names a specific person, place, or thing. Grammar Girl High School would be capitalized because it's a specific high school. Notice in the previous sentence that the second *high school* isn't capitalized because it isn't the name of a specific high school—it's a generic use of the word.

Common Nouns	Proper Nouns
a river	the Passaic River
the doctor	Doctor Horrible

To learn how these general capitalization rules apply to specific words, such as nicknames, planets, seasons, directions, and dog breeds, see Appendix section A-1.

PLURALS: NOUNS, NOUNS EVERYWHERE

You have one computer, but you'd love another one. Easy—at least on paper. Add an *s*. Ta-da! You have two computers (or more). Magic!

It's fairly easy to make nouns plural. The last letter or letters of the word determine what you need to do.

Usually, you just add *s*.

action	actions
hole	holes
pencil	pencils

When the word ends in *ch*, *s*, *sh*, *x*, or *z*, add *es*.

birch	birches
fox	foxes
klutz	klutzes
platypus	platypuses
thrush	thrushes

When the word ends in *y*, look at the letter before *y*. If it's a vowel, add *s*.

holiday	holidays
key	keys

If the letter before *y* is a consonant, change the *y* to *i* and then add *es*.

rally	rallies

Words that end in *o* don't follow specific rules; some words take an *s* to become plural and other words take an *es* to become plural. You have to memorize the spellings.

cello	cellos
echo	echoes
kangaroo	kangaroos
tomato	tomatoes

Except That . . .

If you're dealing with a family name or product name, it doesn't matter what comes before the *y*. Just add an *s*. *Clery* becomes the *Clerys* and *BlackBerry* (the phone) becomes *BlackBerrys*.

Making Abbreviations Plural

Add s to make abbreviations plural, but make sure it's a small s, not a capitalized one (and don't use an apostrophe). The rule is the same regardless of whether the abbreviation has periods.

CD   CDs
DVD   DVDs
M.D. M.D.s

See section 3-34 for how to make single letters plural.

What's UP with That?

Some nouns are called **compound nouns**. Don't panic! All that means is that the noun is made up of more than one word—for example, *brother-in-law*. It's a small collection of words that make up a noun just as a family compound is a collection of buildings that make up a residence.

What's the main noun in *brother-in-law? Brother*, not *law*. The *law* part simply tells you what kind of brother he is. So, you put the s on *brother* when you're talking about two brothers-in-law.

If you came in second place in a track meet, you're the *runner-up.* If you tied for second, you're one of the *runners-up.*

Tricky Nouns: Mouse? Mice? Meese?

With some nouns, you just have to know what the plural is, such as *mice* (for *mouse*), *teeth* (for *tooth*), *deer* (for *deer*), *knives* (for *knife*), *children* (for *child*), and *oxen* (for *ox*). Some of our words retain qualities of Latin or other languages they came from, so their plurals aren't formed in a standard way. Examples include *appendices* (plural of *appendix*), *phenomena* (plural of *phenomenon*), and *bases* (plural of *basis*).

If you're not sure what the plural form of a word is, go to the dictionary. The dictionary is your friend—honest. It will give you the plural of the word if the plural isn't standard.

✓✓ Check It Out ✓✓

Rarely, language experts will say you can choose between two acceptable plural forms of a noun. For example, when you're talking about a computer mouse, the plural can be either *mice* or *mouses*, and although most people who work with plants prefer the plural *cacti*, most dictionaries say either *cacti* or *cactuses* is fine. *Index* becomes *indices* when you're writing about math or science, but in other cases it is usually made plural as *indexes*; and although *buses* is the preferred plural of *bus*, you can also go with *busses*. When in doubt, check a dictionary. The first plural form listed is the one that is most common. ✓

POP QUIZ

Choose the correct sentence from each pair.

1. A. Squiggly knew one of the justices of the peace.
   B. Squiggly knew one of the justice of the peaces.

2. A. Our family holidays are filled with tradition.
   B. Our family holiday's are filled with tradition.

3. A. The crowd threw rotten tomatos.
   B. The crowd threw rotten tomatoes.

4. A. I hardly ever buy DVDs anymore.
   B. I hardly ever buy DVD's anymore.

5. A. I'm glad I'm not old enough to pay taxs.
   B. I'm glad I'm not old enough to pay taxes.

VERBS: READY, CAMERA, ACTION

We have our people, places, and things—nouns—established, but they're not doing anything. We have to get those things, people, and ideas moving. Enter the verb! Verbs add movement to your writing. Like nouns, verbs come in different categories.

TRANSITIVE AND INTRANSITIVE VERBS

The first way you can put verbs in groups is to separate them into transitive and intransitive piles. There's an easy way to remember those names, which I'll get to in a minute.

Transitive verbs take their action on something—the object. If you remove the object from these sentences, they don't make sense:

He will **lay** *the book* on the table.
(*Lay* is the verb; *the book* is the necessary object.)

She **gave** *the pearl* to the wizard.
(*Gave* is the verb; *the pearl* is the necessary object.)

Intransitive verbs don't need an object; they can take action all by themselves. No object is necessary in these sentences:

He ran.
She sits.

The Quick and Dirty Tip to remember what these names mean is to think of a <u>trans</u>itive verb as <u>trans</u>ferring its action to the object. Both *transitive* and *transfer* start with the prefix *trans*.

Some verbs can be transitive or intransitive depending on how they are used.

> They cheered. (intransitive)
> They cheered the team. (transitive)

ACTION VERBS AND LINKING VERBS

1-5

The next way you can put verbs into groups is to sort them into action verbs and linking verbs. Action verbs are exactly what they sound like: they describe actions. Verbs such as *run, jump*, and *swim* are action verbs.

Linking verbs describe a state of being. The action isn't so rugged, but more thoughtful, connective, or complicated. Linking verbs aren't about actions as much as they are about connecting other words together.

The verb *to be* is the basic linking verb. The word *is* is a form of the verb *to be*. If I say, "Squiggly is yellow," the main purpose of *is* is to link the word *Squiggly* with the word *yellow*.

Simple Forms of *To Be*:

	Present	Past
I	am	was
she/he/it	is	was
we/you/they	are	were

See Appendix section A-4 for a complete conjugation of *to be*.

Other linking verbs include *seem, appear, look, become*, and verbs that describe senses, such as *feel* and *smell*. There are at least sixty linking verbs in the English language.

Of course, it can't be as simple as action versus linking verbs. You wouldn't need me if it were.

The complication is that some verbs—such as the sensing verbs—can be both linking verbs and action verbs. A Quick and Dirty Tip to help you figure out whether you're dealing with a linking or an action verb is to see if you can replace the verb with a form of *to be*. If so, then it's probably a linking verb.

> He smells bad. (He has a bad odor.)
> He is bad. (He is ill-behaved.)

In the above sentence, *smells* is a linking verb because if you replace *smells* with the word *is*, the sentence still makes sense. *Bad* describes the noun *he*, not the verb *smells* or *is*.

Now see what happens when *smells* is an action verb.

> He smells badly. (His nose isn't working.)
> He is badly. (This doesn't make sense.)

Replacing *smells* with *is* doesn't work, so you know you have an action verb. *Badly* describes the verb *smells*, not the noun *he*.

Verbs That Are Sometimes Linking Verbs and Sometimes Action Verbs

This list contains the most common words that can be either linking verbs or action verbs. Notice that it's possible to replace the verb with a form of *to be* in each sentence without dramatically changing the meaning.

Verb	Example as a Linking Verb	Test Sentence That Proves It Is a Linking Verb
feel	I feel energetic.	I am energetic.
get	He got fired.	He was fired.
grow	We grow weary.	We are weary.

look	She looks happy.	She is happy.
smell	It smells fragrant.	It is fragrant.
sound	The music sounds loud.	The music is loud.
taste	It tastes salty.	It is salty.

Verb	Example as an Action Verb	Test Sentence That Proves It Is an Action Verb*
feel	He felt the grass.	He was the grass.
get	He got the bike.	He was the bike.
grow	He grew peas.	He was peas.
look	He looked west.	He was west.
prove	He proved it.	He was it.
smell	He smelled the leaf.	He was the leaf.
sound	He sounded the alarm.	He was the alarm.
taste	He tasted the peas.	He was the peas.

* The meaning of the paired sentence changes when you replace the action verb with the linking verb *was*.

VERB TENSES: LIVE FOR TODAY

1-6

People say, "Live for today, forget about yesterday, and ignore tomorrow." But if everyone did live in the now, I wouldn't get to invite you to explore the exciting world of verb tenses.

Fortunately, people dwell on the past and plan for the future; history, for example, by definition, happened in the past. Verbs reflect time, which is why we need tenses.

Verbs come in three varieties—**present**, **past**, and **future**. Today, yesterday, and tomorrow.

> Kilroy is here.
> Kilroy was here.
> Kilroy will be here.

But that's not all. Each verb tense can then be spliced into more categories.

Simple—the end of the action is unknown or unimportant. Things are simple when time isn't important.

The captain swims. (simple present)

Perfect—the action has ended or will end; it is complete or will be completed. It starts. It ends. It's known. It's completed. Things are perfect when you know everything about them.

The captain has swum. (present perfect)

Progressive—the action is ongoing, progressing, or will be ongoing; it is continuous. We have no idea when it will end; it's incomplete.

The captain is swimming. (present progressive)

Perfect Progressive—the action progressed for a while before it ended or before it will end.

The captain has been swimming. (present perfect progressive)

For your reading pleasure, here's a handy chart with all the major verb tenses:

SIMPLE (also called indefinite)	EXAMPLE	MEANING OF SENTENCE
Simple present	Jack walks.	It is a fact that Jack walks.
Simple past	Jack walked.	Jack walked at some point in the past.
Simple future	Jack will walk. Jack is going to walk.	In the future, Jack will go for a walk.
PERFECT (also called complete)	EXAMPLE	MEANING OF SENTENCE
Present perfect	Jack has walked.	Jack finished his walk.
Past perfect	Jack had walked.	In the past, Jack walked, and then he stopped.

Future perfect	Jack will have walked. Jack is going to have walked (three miles before the end of the week).	In the future, Jack will stop walking before something else happens.
PROGRESSIVE (also called incomplete and continuous)	**EXAMPLE**	**MEANING OF SENTENCE**
Present progressive	Jack is walking.	Jack is in the middle of a walk.
Past progressive	Jack was walking.	At some point in the past, Jack was in the middle of a walk, but we don't know when he stopped or if he did.
Future progressive	Jack will be walking. Jack is going to be walking.	Jack will walk in the future— and walk and walk. Who knows when it will end?
PERFECT PROGRESSIVE (also called perfect continuous)	**EXAMPLE**	**MEANING OF SENTENCE**
Present perfect progressive	Jack has been walking.	Jack started walking sometime in the past, and he is still walking. (He may stop now, or he may keep walking.)
Past perfect progressive	Jack had been walking.	At some point in the past, Jack started walking and did so for a while, but now his walk is over.
Future perfect progressive	Jack will have been walking. Jack is going to have been walking (for three hours by the time he reaches the store).	Jack will walk until a specific point in the future, and then he will stop.

These three sentences are all in the simple present tense, but if you consider them, you may notice that they seem different:

I want chocolate. (state present)

Put the chocolate in the bowl. (instantaneous present)

She eats chocolate. (habitual present)

People who describe language, such as the British linguist

Randolph Quirk, also noticed that these sentences are different and gave them categories—the names you see next to the sentences.

Simple present tense verbs can describe a state (wanting, thinking, feeling), an instantaneous action (an instruction, a brief action), or a habit—an ongoing or repeated action (sneezing, editing, reading).

Do you need to know the category names to write well? No. But it's fascinating, and being aware of the different categories can keep you from getting confused when you see a simple present tense verb doing something besides its simplest "Jack walks" job.

Irregular Verbs

Since we're talking about tenses, what's up with past tense verbs like *drew*, *went*, and *flung*? They're called **irregular verbs**. Why aren't the past tense forms *drawed*, *goed*, and *flinged*? Your two-year-old cousin probably thinks they are! That's because kids absorb the rules for forming regular verbs first because regular verbs are the most common verb form.

Regular verbs follow a pattern: you make them past tense by adding *d* or *ed*.

Present Tense	Past Tense
hoe	hoed
jump	jumped

Irregular verbs don't follow that pattern; they are holdovers from the past. Believe it or not, rules for **conjugation** (a fancy word for "working the verb") were even more complicated in the olden days. Let's not even talk about it.

Over time, conjugation rules got simpler and most verbs were regularized. Today, English has fewer than two hundred irregular verbs, but they are some of the most common ones you use.

Present Tense	Past Tense
am	was
do	did
draw	drew
fling	flung
go	went
run	ran
say	said
see	saw
sit	sat

See Common Irregular Verbs in Appendix section A-4 for more examples.

SUBJUNCTIVE VERBS: IF I WERE A RICH GIRL

1-7

Most people don't realize it, but verbs can be as moody as cats. Verbs can be **commanding** (*imperative mood*), **matter-of-fact** (*indicative mood*), or **doubtful** or **wishful** (*subjunctive mood*).

Don't talk to me! (imperative)
Squiggly ate too much. (indicative)
I wish I were a rock star. (subjunctive)

The mood of the verb *to be*, when you use the phrase *I were*, is called the subjunctive mood.

Let's talk a bit more about the subjunctive mood, since it's the most confusing mood. A **subjunctive verb** is used to communicate such feelings as wishfulness, hopefulness, and imagination—things that aren't real or true. For example, when the Cowardly Lion in *The Wizard of Oz* sings "If I were king of the forest," he is fantasizing about all the things he would do if he were brave. He's not courageous—he's just imagining—so *if I were* is the correct statement. *I were* often follows the word *if*, because *if* often means you are wishing or imagining.

In a subjunctive sentence, the verb is often also accompanied by a statement using wishful words like *would* or *could*.

> If Aardvark were famous, his face would be on the one-dollar bill.

1-8 # VERBALS

Verbals may seem to have been designed to confuse you. **Verbals** feel like verbs, but they act like something else in a sentence. There are three types of verbals: *gerunds*, *participles*, and *infinitives*. Gerunds act like nouns, participles act like adjectives, and infinitives can act like nouns, adjectives, or adverbs.

1-9 ## GERUNDS

If you add *ing* to the end of a verb and use that word as a noun, it's called a **gerund**. For example, take the verb *act* and add *ing* to get *acting*. You can use it as the name of a profession—a noun:

> *Acting* isn't as easy as it looks.

Acting is a gerund in that sentence; it functions like a noun. Here are two more sentences with gerunds:

> Aardvark's *singing* almost deafened Squiggly.

> After you finish this book, you will want everyone to read your *writing*.

1-10 ## PARTICIPLES

If you add *ing* to the end of a verb and use that word as an adjective (see section 1-24), then it's called a **participle**. Let's use *acting* again.

> *Acting* lessons helped Aardvark land the lead role in the school play.

Acting is a participle in that sentence; it functions like an adjective by describing the noun *lessons*.

Adding *ing* to regular verbs makes present participles, and adding *d, ed, n, en,* or *t* to regular verbs makes past participles.

The *fallen* leaves made a striking pattern.

INFINITIVES

1-11

An **infinitive** is a combination of the word *to* and a bare form of a verb: *to go, to run, to split,* and so on.

To act was his secret desire.
(infinitive as noun)

It is his time *to shine.*
(infinitive as adjective: *to shine* modifies *time*)

He sprinted the last 10 yards *to secure* the win.
(infinitive as adverb: *to secure* modifies *sprinted*)

Splitting Infinitives: Splitsville

I know it may come as a surprise, but I, Grammar Girl, am not that adventurous. My idea of fun? Splitting infinitives. Sometimes I split them when I don't have to just because I can. Yeah, that's my idea of fun!

To understand my thrill, you have to know that some people believe it's against the "rules" to split an infinitive. I consider it my calling to dispel that myth.

Blame Latin for the logic behind the 19th-century rule about not splitting infinitives. In Latin there are no two-word infinitives, so it's impossible to split one. Early on, many English teachers decided that because infinitives couldn't be split in Latin, they shouldn't be split in English either.

But notions change over time, and today almost everyone

agrees that it is OK to split infinitives, especially when you would have to change the meaning of the sentence or go through writing gymnastics to avoid the split.

Here's an example of a sentence with a split infinitive:

Squiggly decided to quickly remove Aardvark's cats.

In this case, the word *quickly* splits the infinitive *to remove*: *to quickly remove*.

If you try to unsplit the verb, you might actually change the meaning. For example, you might say

Squiggly decided quickly to remove Aardvark's cats.

Now you've left the infinitive intact, but instead of saying that Squiggly quickly removed Aardvark's cats (zip zip) while Aardvark stepped out for a minute, you're saying Squiggly made a decision quickly.

You could rewrite the sentence without the split infinitive and not lose the original meaning.

Squiggly decided to remove Aardvark's cats quickly.

That could be an even better sentence, but from a grammatical standpoint, rewriting isn't necessary.

Bottom line? You can usually avoid splitting infinitives if you want to, but the only reason to do so is that there are a few hold-outs who think it's wrong. If you're worried about being judged by a stickler, you can avoid split infinitives, but if you have a chance to defend yourself, talk to the sticklers about the silly Latin origin of the rule, and don't let them tell you that splitting infinitives is forbidden.

QUICK AND DIRTY TIP

If you want to remember what a split infinitive is, just remember what may be the most famous example: *Star Trek*'s "to boldly go where no one has gone before." *To* <u>boldly go</u> is a split infinitive. Yup, I'm a *Star Trek* fan, but I'll never boldly go into space; splitting infinitives is about as crazy as I get.

PRONOUNS

1-12

Personal pronouns stand in for nouns. They're like stuntmen. When nouns feel overworked, they call for pronouns—words like *he*, *it*, *she*, *we*, *they*, and so on. The noun to which a pronoun refers is called its **antecedent**. Because pronouns don't get the same recognition as the big stars, they're a little temperamental. It's their way of getting even.

Squiggly was late. <u>He</u> forgot to set an alarm.

The tree fell because <u>it</u> had been attacked by bugs.

Grammar Girl is happy that <u>she</u> remembered to bring an eraser.

Pronouns are vital. Try not using one for an hour, and you'll see. I use them constantly, as you can tell by these sentences.

Because pronouns come in different "shapes" and are used for different reasons, some official grammar language is necessary. Ready?

1-13

PRONOUNS AND THEIR CASES

Pronouns are bunched together into three cases. (I don't know why the word *case* is used. *Categories* would work just as well, but officially they're called cases.) Think of each case as a suitcase; it packs all the similar pronouns together.

PRONOUNS IN THEIR SUITCASES			
PERSON	SUBJECTIVE CASE	OBJECTIVE CASE	POSSESSIVE CASE (weak/strong)
1st Person	I	Me	My/Mine
2nd Person	You	You	Your/Yours
3rd Person—female	She	Her	Her/Hers
3rd Person—male	He	Him	His/His
3rd Person—neutral	It	It	Its/Its
1st Person (plural)	We	Us	Our/Ours
2nd Person (plural)	You	You	Your/Yours
3rd Person (plural)	They	Them	Their/Theirs
Interrogative	Who	Whom	Whose

Subjective Case—the doer of the action; the one who acts

She ate fifty hot dogs.

(*She* did the eating, so she's taking the action.)

Objective Case—the receiver of the action; the one who sits back and lets it all happen to her (or him)

The judge gave <u>her</u> the prize.
(*Her* received the prize and is the receiver of the action—giving.)

Possessive Case—shows ownership

<u>Her</u> dog threw up on my shoes.
(*Her* indicates the dog belongs to a previously mentioned female.)

First person tells the story from the point of view of the person who is talking. You're being told the story by one person, and you're in that person's mind.

I often wonder what my dog is thinking.

Second person directs the text to you, the reader. It's usually used in nonfiction, such as this book.

Try not using a pronoun for an hour. See if you can.

Third person observes the story from the outside. The narrator can let you know what is happening in different people's thoughts and can follow different characters.

Sarah hates cats, so she was surprised to find one in her room.

Authors often write novels in first person or third person; they rarely use second person.

You and I Are Going to the Beach

Some pronouns will work only when they are in charge (subjective case), and other pronouns will work only when they can be lazy and just receive the action (objective case). Subjects are the ones initiating action in a sentence, and objects are the ones having action taken on them. For example, *I* is exclusively a subject pronoun, whereas *me* is exclusively an object pronoun.

<u>I</u> threw the beach ball.

(*I* is the subject taking the action.)

Squiggly threw <u>me</u>.

(*Me* is the object getting thrown.)

On the other hand, *you* has to stand in for everyone! *You* gets called to the set whether the scene needs a subject or an object.

<u>You</u> threw the beach ball.

(*You* is the subject taking the action.)

Squiggly threw <u>you</u>.

(*You* is the object getting thrown.)

You also fills in for one person or many people (i.e., it's a singular and a plural pronoun). If I say "You should go to Disneyland," I could be talking to one person or a group of people. *You* could be standing in for Squiggly alone or Squiggly, Aardvark, and their families.

POSSESSIVE PRONOUNS: YOURS, MINE, AND OURS

Whether you've seen the remake from 2005 or the original from 1968, you know what the title of the movie *Yours, Mine, and Ours* means. Ownership. It means all those kids belong to one another and to both parents.

Grammarians like the word *possessive* (which seems more selfish than the word *belonging*, but I am not here to judge).

Some possessive pronouns can stand alone, such as *mine, yours, his, hers, ours,* and *theirs.* Some people call these **strong possessive pronouns**.

> The cat is hers.

Some possessive pronouns (such as *my, your, his, her, our,* and *their*) need a noun. Some people call these **weak possessive pronouns**, and other people call them **possessive adjectives**.

> That is *her* cat.

If you go back and look at the last chart, you'll notice that *his* is on both lists. *His* is both the strong and weak possessive form of *he,* meaning you can write both *The cat is his* and *That is his cat.* The same is true of *its,* although it would be rare to write a sentence using *its* as a strong possessive pronoun.

The most astute readers will also have realized that sentences can be made in which *her* doesn't need a noun, such as *He went with her.* Again, if you look at the chart, you'll see that *her* is both an object pronoun and a weak possessive pronoun. In the sentence *That is her cat,* it's being used as a possessive pronoun and needs a noun. In the sentence *He went with her,* it's being used as an object pronoun and doesn't need a noun.

Gerunds and Possessive Pronouns

You remember gerunds, right? They are those verbs we talked

about in section 1-9 that become nouns by adding an *ing*. Gerunds usually need a possessive pronoun.

> Aardvark thought **him** singing was atrocious. (nope)
> Aardvark thought **his** singing was atrocious. (yup)

The first sentence sounds wrong, but there are situations when choosing between a possessive pronoun and an objective pronoun changes the sentence.

> We didn't know that was **his** singing.

That sentence means we couldn't tell if what he was doing was singing or making some other kind of noise.

When we use an objective pronoun, the sentence means something different.

> We didn't know that was **him** singing.

Now the writer is saying it could have been someone else singing. It was definitely singing; the writer just didn't know who was doing it.

Here's one last set of examples.

> Do you mind **my** leaving?
> Do you mind **me** leaving?

In the first example, with the possessive pronoun *my*, you want to know if the reader is bothered by your action of leaving. Leaving is the thing you're asking about.

In the second example, with the objective pronoun *me*, you want to know if the reader is bothered by you when you are leaving. That's why gerunds usually take possessive pronouns: when you use a gerund, it's usually the action you want to know about, not the person or thing.

POP QUIZ

Which sentence is correct?

1. Him looking cool mattered less to his mother than to him.
2. His looking cool mattered less to his mother than to him.
3. He looking cool mattered less to his mother than to him.

Answer: 2

INDEFINITE PRONOUNS

1-15

Indefinite pronouns, such as *everyone* and *anybody*, represent an indefinite number of nouns. They often sound like a lot of people but are usually treated as singular.

> <u>Everyone</u> is wondering what Squiggly is doing here.
> <u>Anybody</u> can see that the skating rink is closed.

DEMONSTRATIVE PRONOUNS

1-16

The words *this*, *that*, *these*, and *those* are called **demonstrative pronouns** when they are acting like nouns and you can imagine pointing at something when you use them.

> <u>That</u> is the ticket I lost.
> <u>Those</u> are my favorite shoes.

These words can also be adjectives when they come right before a noun.

> <u>That</u> ticket had been lost for days!

RECIPROCAL PRONOUNS

1-17

The **reciprocal pronouns** are *each other* and *one another*. They refer to the members of a larger group.

Squiggly and Aardvark gave <u>each other</u> coffee mugs.

The chess team gave <u>one another</u> high-fives for winning the tournament.

1-18

COMBINING PRONOUNS: THREE DOESN'T HAVE TO BE A CROWD.

For some reason, people who know how to behave when they are alone get flustered when other people show up in their sentences. Don't let company in your sentences make you go all atwitter.

I know none of you would ever say "Me love Squiggly" instead of "I love Squiggly."

Yet throw in a third party, and I bet some of you would say "My brother and me love Squiggly."

My brother and me love Squiggly is wrong for the same reason that *Me love Squiggly* is wrong: you're putting an object pronoun (*me*) in the subject position. The correct sentence uses the subject pronoun in the active (or subject) position.

My brother and I love Squiggly.

Writers can have the same problem when two or more people become the object in a sentence. Would any of you really say "Father loves he"? I hope not! You'd correctly say "Father loves him." But again, you get a little sister, and suddenly everyone forgets how to construct a sentence. It's not *Father loves she and Squiggly*. Remember: object pronouns go in the object position. *Father loves her and Squiggly* is correct.

Just Between You and Me, You and I Know How to Have Fun
Sometimes even people who can deal with crowds in their sentences get confused when *you* shows up.

The reason it gets a little tricky when you combine other pronouns with *you* is that *you* is both a subject and an object pronoun. *You love Squiggly*, and *Squiggly loves you. You and he should go scuba diving*, and *I went scuba diving with you and her.* They are all correct.

So now that we've got *you* straight, we can move on to *between you and I* and figure out why it's wrong.

I'm going to have to talk about **prepositions** before we've officially covered them. If this makes you uncomfortable, hum loudly or cover your ears while you read this next short section. Then, once you've read about prepositions later (see section 1-30), you can reread this section (without the humming) and be assured that you are one with prepositions and pronouns.

Between is a preposition, just as *at, above, over,* and *including* are prepositions. Because prepositions usually either describe a relationship or show possession, they don't act alone; they often answer questions like *Where?* and *When?* For example, if I say "Keep that secret between you and me," *between* describes where the secret is to be kept. If I say "I'll tell you the secret at dinnertime," *at* describes when the secret will be revealed.

So, instead of acting alone, prepositions are part of prepositional phrases. In those example sentences, *between you and me* and *at dinnertime* are prepositional phrases. And it's just a rule that pronouns following prepositions in those phrases are always in the objective case. You have to memorize it. When you're using the objective case, the correct pronoun is *me*, so the correct prepositional phrase is *between you and me*. (If it helps, you can remember that the Jessica Simpson song "Between You and I" is wrong, so wrong.)

What's UP with That?

Pronouns following a preposition are always in the objective case; they will always be *me*, *you*, *him*, *her*, *it*, *them*, or *us*. Don't even question it! It's just a rule—one to memorize.

Most grammarians are often sympathetic to people who say "between you and I" because it's considered a hypercorrection. You might feel funny writing *between you and me*, but be brave; be strong. Between you and me, we know we're right!

POP QUIZ

Which sentence is correct?

1. Between us, us will find the buried treasure.
2. Between we, we will find the buried treasure.
3. Between you and I, we will find the buried treasure.
4. Between you and me, we will find the buried treasure.

Answer: 4

Some people seem afraid to use the word *me*. Another hypercorrection that avoids *me* (like incorrectly saying *between you and I*) is throwing *myself* into a sentence when you are unsure or want to sound refined.

Let's dissect what's wrong with this sentence: *Please call Aardvark or myself with questions*. Once more, you've run into the problem of having multiple people in the sentence.

Step back and consider how you would say the sentence without Aardvark. Obviously, you would say "Please call me with questions," not "Please call myself with questions."

You use *me* because the objective case (*me*) receives the action of being called.

Adding Aardvark doesn't change anything. It's still correct to say "Please call Aardvark or me with questions."

Myself is what's called a **reflexive pronoun**. Just think about looking into a mirror and seeing your reflection. You'd say "I see myself in the mirror." You see your reflection, and *myself* is called a reflexive pronoun.

Other reflexive pronouns are *himself, herself, yourself, itself, ourselves*, and *themselves*. A reflexive pronoun can only be the object of a sentence; it can never be the subject. You would never say "Myself stepped on Squiggly," so you would also never say "Aardvark and myself stepped on Squiggly."

The reflexive pronoun is the right choice when the subject is mentioned again in the sentence. For example, you can use *myself* when you are both the subject and the object of a sentence: *I see myself playing maracas* or *I'm going to treat myself to a mud bath*. In both cases, you are the object of your own action, so *myself* is the right word to use.

Reflexive pronouns can also be used to add emphasis to a sentence. (In case you care, they are then called **intensive pronouns**.) For example, if you saw a stuntman crash on the set, you could say

"I myself saw the horrible crash." Sure, it's a tad dramatic, but it's grammatically correct. If you want to emphasize how proud you are of a song you wrote, you could say "I wrote the song myself." Again, *myself* just adds emphasis. The meaning of the sentence doesn't change if you take out the word *myself*; it just has a different feeling because it lacks the added emphasis.

1-20 ## *THEY* AS A SINGULAR PRONOUN: THE SINGLE LIFE

Let's say you're writing a sentence that starts **When a student succeeds** . . .

At that point you're probably confused about how you should finish the sentence when you're talking about one unknown person.

Which of the following would you use?

> *he* should thank *his* teacher.
> *she* should thank *her* teacher.
> *he or she* should thank *his or her* teacher.
>
> or
>
> *they* should thank *their* teacher.

It's either an awkward sentence or an incorrect use of plurals with singulars—it's a "tear your hair out" situation!

Honestly, I don't think there is a perfect solution, and I would like to avoid the question because I know that no matter what I say, I'm going to make someone angry. Many grammarians have a hard time agreeing on this as well.

I will state for the record that I am a firm believer that someday *they* will be the acceptable choice for this situation. English currently lacks an appropriate word, and many people are already either mistakenly or purposely using *they* as a singular gender-neutral pronoun. It seems logical that rules will eventually move in that direction.

Some grammarians, including me, already allow people to use *they* and *them* as a singular pronoun when the sex of the subject is unknown.

But not everyone agrees. At this point, since Grammar Girl isn't especially brave, I usually ask myself if there is any way to avoid the problem. Most of the time it's easy to simply make the original noun plural. You could say *When students [plural] succeed, they should thank their teachers*. Sometimes more extensive rewriting is required, and if necessary, I'll do it. I would rewrite a whole paragraph if it meant I could avoid the problem.

Rewriting is almost always possible, but if it isn't, then you have to make a choice. If I'm writing a formal document, I'll use *he or she*. For example, *When a person wins an election, he or she should thank his or her volunteers*. Admittedly, it's a little awkward, but if you're already using formal language, I don't think it's too distracting.

It takes a bold, confident, and possibly reckless person to use *they* with a singular pronoun today. If you do it, you'll be in the company of such revered authors as Jane Austen, Lewis Carroll, and Shakespeare. But if there's a chance that one of your teachers would think you are careless or ignorant of the "rule," then don't.

The Quick and Dirty Tip is to rewrite your sentences to avoid the problem. If that's not possible, ask your teacher if they (look at me being brave!) have a preference.

If not, use *he or she* if you want to play it safe, or use *they* if you feel bold and prepared to defend yourself.

IT IS I, GRAMMAR GIRL

1-21

How should you respond to the question "Who is there?"

It's proper to respond, "It is I."

When people call me and ask, "May I speak to Grammar Girl?" I properly respond, "This is she."

The traditional grammar rule states that when a pronoun follows a linking verb such as *is* it should be in the subjective case. That means it is correct to say "It is I" and "It was he who dropped the phone in shock when I answered 'This is she.'"

When pronouns follow these non-action verbs, you use subject pronouns, such as *I*, *she*, *he*, *they*, and *we*.

Here are some additional correct examples:

> Who called Squiggly? It was he.
> Who told you about it? It was I.
> Who had the phone conversation? It must have been they.

Now, the problem is that 90 percent of you are almost certainly thinking, "That all sounds really weird. Is she serious?" Well, yes, I'm serious. That is the traditional rule, but fortunately, most grammarians forgive you for not following the rule because it sounds stilted and fussy, even to us.

So if you're the kind of person who prefers to be proper (or you want to mess with people), it's fine to say "It is I," and if you prefer to be more casual, it's fine to say "It is me."

If you have a teacher who demands the correct use of a subjective pronoun after a linking verb, then that is what you should use.

POP QUIZ

Fill in the blanks.

1. I _____ didn't realize that _____ dancing
   me or **myself**   **she** or **her**

   was _____ way of expressing _____ .
        her's or **her**   **her** or **herself**

2. It is _____ .
          our or **ours**

3. It is _____ .
          my or **mine**

4. Squiggly and _____ gave _____ a surprise party.
     I or **me** or **us**   **he** or **him**

5. _____ wanted _____ week to be sunny.
   Everyone or **them**   **this** or **those**

RELATIVE AND INTERROGATIVE PRONOUNS

Finally, there are two more classes of pronouns:

Relative pronouns (*that, which, who, whom, whose*) introduce subordinate clauses, which you will learn about in chapter two.

> Here is a tree <u>that</u> fell on my car.
> She is the girl <u>who</u> won the spelling bee.

Interrogative pronouns (*what, which, who, whom, whose*) introduce questions:

> <u>Who</u> went to the party?
> <u>Which</u> car did you take?

ADJECTIVES AND ADVERBS: MODIFIERS

You have your nouns, verbs, and pronouns, but how do you add color and texture to those words? With modifiers, of course! They describe or make something specific.

Adjectives and adverbs are **modifiers**—the parts of speech that describe nouns, verbs, pronouns, and in some cases one another.

ADJECTIVES

An adjective describes a noun (or a pronoun) by telling you which one, what kind, or how many. The words can be as vague as *this*, *huge*, and *some*, or they can be as specific as *soft*, *twelve*, and *wet*.

> Aardvark threw <u>some</u> pillows at Squiggly.
> Aardvark threw a <u>square</u> pillow at Squiggly.

1-25

ADVERBS

The adverb works harder than the adjective. It can describe verbs, adjectives, other adverbs, clauses, and whole sentences. You can easily remember the connection between adverbs and verbs because the word *verb* is inside the word *adverb*. Then note that adverbs are busy like verbs because they modify a bunch of other things too. Something that is active (like an adverb) can cover a lot of ground (other parts of speech).

> Squiggly <u>deftly</u> dodged the pillows.
> (The adverb *deftly* modifies the verb *dodged*.)

> Squiggly <u>quite</u> deftly dodged the pillows.
> (The adverb *quite* modifies the adverb *deftly*, which itself modifies the verb *dodged*.)

> Squiggly dodged the <u>unusually</u> hard pillow.
> (The adverb *unusually* modifies the adjective *hard*, which modifies the noun *pillow*.)

The adverb tells you *where*, *when*, and *how* (how often and how much). An adverb can be as vague as *now*, *then*, *sometimes*, and *hardly*, or it can be as precise as *inside*, *today*, *coldly*, or *hourly*.

Adverbs often end in *ly*, but not always.

1-26

WORDS THAT CAN BE ADJECTIVES OR ADVERBS

Just to make things a little confusing, there are some words that can be adverbs or adjectives depending on how they are used in a sentence. You can always tell the difference by noting what the word is modifying. If it's modifying a noun, then the word is an adjective; if it's modifying something else, such as a verb, then the word is an adverb.

Adjective	Adverb
He kept a <u>weekly</u> calendar.	He jogged <u>weekly</u>.
They made it a <u>late</u> night.	He stayed <u>late</u>.
The <u>hard</u> nails worked.	He worked <u>hard</u>.

LINKING VERBS WITH ADJECTIVES AND ADVERBS: THE MISSING LINK

1-27

Remember linking verbs from section 1-5? When you're dealing with sensing verbs, such as *taste*, *smell*, *look*, or *feel*, you have to take a minute to decide whether you're describing the noun or the verb.

Consider the different meanings of these two sentences:

I feel bad.
I feel badly.

It's correct to say "I feel bad" when expressing an emotion. You just hurt your friend's feelings, so you feel bad about it. *Bad* describes your state of mind. It's an adjective describing the pronoun *I*. Remember to test the sentence by replacing the verb with a form of *to be*. *I am bad* works, so you know *feels* is a linking verb in the sentence.

When you say "I feel *badly*," the adverb *badly* describes the action verb *feel*. Since the action verb *feel* can imply "to touch things," *feeling badly* can imply that something is wrong with your sense of touch.

I know that people think they need to describe how they feel, so they use an adverb by mistake. It's those pesky linking verbs that cause such confusion. Don't fall into the sinking linking-verb quicksand.

Use adverbs with action verbs. For example, if you gave a horrible speech, you could say, "I spoke badly," because *spoke* is an action verb. You can tell that because speaking is an action, and the test sentence *I am badly* doesn't work.

With sense verbs, first test whether they are linking verbs or action verbs. Then use my adjective-adverb Quick and Dirty Tip:

QUICK AND DIRTY TIP

Adjectives follow linking verbs.
Adverbs modify action verbs.

Good Versus *Well*

A simple question can send people into a panic: How are you?

Do you say "I'm well" or "I'm good"?

Isn't it safer to shrug?

You needn't panic any longer.

"I'm good" is what you're likely to hear, but some grammar nit-pickers will tell you that *well* is an adverb (and therefore modifies verbs) and that *good* is an adjective (and therefore modifies nouns), but the situation isn't that simple (and people think brain surgery is complicated!).

The wonderful news is that it's perfectly acceptable to say "I'm good."

The nitpickers don't understand that the linking verb is the key, but you do.

Adjectives describe nouns and pronouns. *I* is a pronoun. *Am* is a linking verb. Adjectives follow linking verbs. *Good* is an adjective.

I am good is good!

(Adjectives actually have a special name when they follow linking verbs in this way; they're called predicate adjectives. See section 2-2.)

I can hear some of you insisting that you were taught to use *well*, as in "I am well."

Well can be both an adverb and a predicate adjective. When you say "I am well," you're using *well* as a predicate adjective. But it's better to use *well* when you're talking about your health. So if you are recovering from an illness and someone is inquiring about your health, it's appropriate to say "I am well." If you're describing your-self on a generally good day and nobody's asking specifically about your health, a more appropriate response is "I am good." But watch out! This is something a lot of people don't understand, but they think they do and get all upset about it. Be prepared to be corrected no matter what you say. And then you can impress people with your knowledge of linking verbs and action verbs.

COMPARATIVES AND SUPERLATIVES: HOW BIG IS BIG? `1-28`

Sometimes you need to compare one noun to another noun or one verb to another verb. Comparing is the job of adjectives and adverbs.

You already know how to use an adjective for one noun and an adverb for one verb.

> It was a <u>peculiar</u> choice.
> Squiggly chose the <u>tall</u> tree.
> Aardvark ran <u>fast</u>.

When you're comparing items, you need to notice whether you're comparing two things or more than two things.

When you compare two items, you use what's called a **comparative**.

You can remember that comparatives are for two things because *comparative* has the sound *pair* in it, and a pair is always two things. It's not spelled like *pair*, but it sounds like *pair*.

For comparatives, use *more* before the adjective or adverb, or the suffix *er* on the end of it.

> more peculiar (It was the more peculiar choice, given the limited options.)
>
> taller (Aardvark chose the taller tree of the remaining pair.)
>
> faster (Squiggly ran faster than Aardvark.)

When you compare three or more items, you're using a **superlative**. You can remember that superlatives are for more than two things because *superlative* has the word *super* in it, and when you want a whole bunch of something, you supersize it.

With superlatives, use *most* before the adjective or adverb, or the suffix *est* on the end of the adjective or adverb.

> most peculiar (It was the most peculiar choice of the day.)
> tallest (Someone else had already chosen the tallest tree.)
> fastest (Bob ran fastest.)

QUICK AND DIRTY TIP

Use a comparative when you have a pair of things and a superlative when you have a supersized group (three or more). If you can use the suffixes *er* or *est*, here's a tip for choosing between them:

When comparing two things, use *er*—it has two letters.

When comparing three or more things, use *est*—it has three letters.

But how do you know whether to use *er* or *more*? *est* or *most*? Generally, the way you choose depends on how many syllables the word has.

Comparisons involving words with one syllable or three or more syllables follow clear rules. We'll get to tricky two-syllable words in a moment.

One-Syllable Words

One-syllable words use the suffixes *er* or *est* on the end. For example, *smart* has one syllable, so you might say "I am smarter than my sister, but I'm not the smartest in the family." It would sound odd to say "I am more smart than my sister, but I'm not the most smart in the family."

Sometimes people ask about *fun*. Technically, it's not an adjective, so you shouldn't use "funner" or "funnest." See the Grammar Girl website for a full explanation.

Three-Syllable Words

Words with three or more syllables use *more* or *most* in front of them. For example, with the four-syllable adjective *spectacular*, you use *more* or *most*, as in "That is the most spectacular painting I've ever seen!" *Spectacularer* would be wrong (and difficult to pronounce).

Two-Syllable Words

The adjectives *tricky* and *careful* have two syllables, so do you say *trickier* or *more tricky*? *Carefulest* or *most careful*? (Answer: *trickier* and *most careful*.)

With two-syllable words, sometimes you use the suffixes, other times you use *more* or *most*, and in some cases you can use either one. The box on the next page has one rule you can follow.

QUICK AND DIRTY TIP

Two-syllable adjectives that end in *y*, *ow*, or *le* can take the suffixes *er* and *est*.

Remember that by thinking they're y-ow-le howl-ey!

Y-ow-le.

Or better yet, think that they are yowli*er* and howli*er* than everything else, and follow the rule that you end them with *er* (or *est*).

mell<u>ow</u>	**mellower**	**mellowest**
subt<u>le</u>	**subtler**	**subtlest**

With words ending in *y*, change the *y* to *i*.

funn<u>y</u>	**funnier**	**funniest**

If you have a two-syllable adjective that doesn't end in *y*, *ow*, or *le* (if it's not yowlier), you'll need to rely on your ear or your dictionary.

"Tear Your Hair Out" Exception

Sometimes, though, no rule will help you determine which way to make a comparison. Some two-syllable adjectives can go both ways. You can say *commoner* or *more common* and *stupider* or *more stupid*.

Less and Least

The comparisons so far have all involved a greater amount of something. When you're talking about not as much, you use *less* and *least* in front of adjectives or adverbs, no matter how many syllables the words have.

For example, you might admit, "I am less athletic than my best friend," or, if you're using an adverb, you could lament, "My sister is the least grammatically oriented person I know."

What's UP with That?

Yup, even adjectives and adverbs can be irregular.

Adjective	Comparative	Superlative
bad	worse	worst
good	better	best
little	less	least
many	more	most
much	more	most

Adverb	Comparative	Superlative
badly	worse	worst
well	better	best

Less Is More

When comparing, choose the simplest way to say something. Sure, writing "The students on the track team run least slow" is correct. But the clearer way to write this is "The students on the track team run fastest."

Know When to Stop

Some adjectives can't be topped. You can't be the most last, the bestest student, the onliest person left on the planet (although if you are, no one will know, so you can make up your own grammar rules). Here are some adjectives that shouldn't be made comparative or superlative:

best	first	only	worst
dead	last	unique	

Sometimes you will hear these words used "improperly" in idioms such as *deader than a doornail*.

POP QUIZ

Fill in the blanks.

1. After five days in the closet, my science experiment smelled _____ .
    terrible or **terribly**

2. Because of his cold, he smelled _____ .
    poor or **poorly**

3. Squiggly's trophy for _____ painting was a
    best or **better**

    _____ paintbrush than Aardvark's, who
    bigger or **biggest**

    got a _____ one for third prize.
    smaller or **more small**

4. The test was _____ than Aardvark
    complicateder or **more complicated**

    thought it would be. He was sure he was the

    _____ one in the class who would get the
    onliest or **only**

    _____ mark.
    lower or **lowest** or **most low**

5. Grammar Girl knew the _____ about grammar
   much or **most**

   in her family except for her _____ niece.
   more smart or **smarter**

6. Squiggly ran _____.
   fastly or **quickly**

ARTICLES ARE A TYPE OF ADJECTIVE: DEFINITE AND INDEFINITE ARTICLES

Articles—*a*, *an*, and *the*—appear in front of nouns, making the noun specific or nonspecific. They are a type of adjective.

A and *an* are called **indefinite articles**.

The is called a **definite article**.

The difference is that *a* and *an* don't say anything special about the word that follows.

For example, think about the sentence *I need a bike*. This means you need any bike, not a specific one.

On the other hand, if you say "I need *the* bike," you want a specific bike, or perhaps you want the only bike that is available. (Still, it's a specific bike.) That's why *the* is called a definite article—you want something definite. That's how I remember the name.

Whether you use *a* or *an* depends on the word that comes next. You use *a* before words that start with a consonant *sound* and *an* before words that start with a vowel *sound*.

Squiggly wanted a bike.
Aardvark wanted an owl.

Remember it's the first sound of the next word that determines whether you choose *a* or *an*, not the first letter of the next word.

> Squiggly waited for <u>an</u> hour.
> Aardvark was on <u>a</u> historic expedition.

An hour is correct because *hour* starts with a vowel sound. People seem to most commonly get tripped up by words that begin with the letters *h*, *u*, and *o*, because sometimes these start with vowel sounds and sometimes they start with consonant sounds. For example, it is *a historic expedition* because *historic* starts with an *h* sound, but it is *an honorable fellow* because *honorable* starts with an *o* sound.

> Squiggly had <u>a</u> Utopian idea.
> (*Utopian* starts with a consonant *y* sound.)

> Aardvark reminded him it's <u>an</u> unfair world.
> (*Unfair* starts with a vowel *u* sound.)

Usually you put *an* before words that start with *o*, but sometimes you use *a*. For example, you would use *a* in the following sentence:

> She has a one-track mind.
> (*One-track* starts with a *w* sound.)

Initialisms beginning with consonants that sound like vowels also require *an.*

> an FM radio
> an LSAT study guide
> an MBA
> an NFL football team

Other letters can also be pronounced either way. Just remember it is the *sound* that governs whether you use *a* or *an*, not the first letter of the word.

PREPOSITIONS: OVER THE MOON 1-30

Remember the example from section 1-18 when I told you that I'd explain prepositions later? It's later now! Prepositions. You've heard of them. You've used them. Maybe you've even misused them. But what are they?

Prepositions create a relationship between words. They're usually short words like *to*, *from*, and *under*; but they can also be longer words such as *through*, *during*, and *between*. It's been said that prepositions often deal with space and time (which always makes me think of *Star Trek*). For example, the prepositions *above*, *by*, and *over* all say something about a position in space; the prepositions *before*, *after*, and *since* all say something about time. There are a whole slew of prepositions, too many to name one by one, so let's just clap for them at the end of this section.

QUICK AND DIRTY TIP

When you see a small word and are not sure if it's a preposition, remember that prepositions are not usually followed by verbs.

ENDING WITH PREPOSITIONS: MYTH-UNDERSTOOD 1-31

Have you ever felt that no one understood you? That others had a label for you that didn't fit? That you knew where you belonged, but people kept insisting on placing you elsewhere?

Welcome to the world of the preposition—a part of speech that often wants to be at the end of the sentence but has to deal with people who were taught that prepositions aren't allowed there.

Those people are perpetuating a myth because nearly all

grammarians agree that it's fine to end sentences with prepositions, at least in some cases.

Here's an example of a sentence that can end with a preposition:

What did you step on?

You can't say "What did you step?" You need to say "What did you step *on*?" to make a proper sentence. If you leave off the *on*, the sentence doesn't make sense.

I can hear some of you thinking, "What about saying, 'On what did you step?'"

Now, I'm all for rewriting, but have you ever heard anyone talk that way? No!

Yes, you could say "On what did you step?" but not even grammarians think you should. It sounds awkward.

On the other hand, some sentences that end in a preposition can be rewritten so that they make sense, say what you want, don't sound convoluted, and don't end in a preposition. Go for it!

The bottom line is that many people think it's wrong to end a sentence with a preposition, so I wouldn't advise doing it in critical situations. Let's say you have a teacher who hates prepositions at the end of the sentence. Try your hardest not to use a preposition there. Rewriting is your friend.

What is ice cream made of? (acceptable)
What are the ingredients in ice cream? (better)

Sometimes you just want to get a good grade rather than fight against silly grammar myths. (But a teacher may also be impressed that you've thought about grammar and writing enough to know a grammar myth.)

If the sentence doesn't work without the preposition, keep it in. And it's usually OK to end with a preposition if the preposition is necessary and the sentence would sound awkward when rewritten.

Even though it's sometimes allowed, don't get carried away; you can't *always* end sentences with prepositions. When you can leave off the preposition and it won't change the meaning, leave it off. Here's an example of a sentence you have probably heard:

Where is she at? (wrong)

Oh, the horror! That is one of the instances where it's not OK to end a sentence with a preposition! The problem is that *Where is she at?* doesn't need the preposition. *Where is she?* means the same thing, so the *at* is unnecessary.

FYI

This would be a good time to tell you that anyone who cares about grammar has issues.

When I say "issues," I mean pet peeves. I have a number of them myself. It seems to come with the territory of delving into grammar and caring about writing.

It's always good to know if your teacher has certain writing demands or preferences.

PREPOSITIONS IN EXCESS: GO OUT OF THE DOOR, HOP ACROSS TO THE SIDEWALK, AND SPIN OFF INTO SPACE

You won't find unnecessary prepositions only at the ends of sentences. People often throw an extraneous preposition into the middle of a sentence, and they shouldn't. Instead of saying "Squiggly jumped *off of the dock*," it's better to say "Squiggly jumped *off the dock*." See? You don't need to say *off of the dock*; *off the dock* says the same thing without the extra word. (An exception is *a couple of*. That's the right way to say it; it's considered an idiom.)

1-32

PREPOSITIONS AND PHRASAL VERBS

Here's another situation where you can end a sentence with a preposition:

> I hope he cheers up.

Up is a preposition, and there it is at the end of the sentence. Why is that OK?

I hope he cheers has a different meaning from *I hope he cheers up.* I hope he cheers whom? The football team? His grandmother? It's difficult to rewrite the sentence:

> Up cheers he I hope. (I hope not!)

So why is the original sentence correct? Because it has a specific meaning. *Cheer up* is what's called a **phrasal verb**—a set of words (a phrase) that acts as a single verb unit. A phrasal verb can have a different meaning from the way the words are used individually. For example, the verb *cheer up* specifically means to become

happier, not to shout upward. Given that *cheer up* is a unit—a phrasal verb—some people don't believe you've ended a sentence with a preposition when you say "I hope he cheers up." They'd say you've ended the sentence with a phrasal verb.

And you'd say, modestly, "Yes, thank you, I know."

When a phrasal verb is transitive (it does its action to something or someone), you can often split the two parts of the verb, but you usually can't when the verb is intransitive (it doesn't act on anything):

> The chicken on the field held up the game.

> The chicken on the field held the game up.
> (The phrasal verb is split, but the sentence is still OK.)

> He dropped out of school.

> He dropped school out of.
> (You can't split this intransitive phrasal verb and still make sense. *Of school* is a prepositional phrase, not an object.)

Other Phrasal Verbs

A verb-plus-preposition combo can create a different meaning from the verb and preposition separately.

look up	run into	sleep over
make up	show up	throw up
run away		

PREPOSITIONAL PHRASES: IT'S JUST A PHASE!

1-34

Prepositions often answer questions like *Where?* and *When?* They usually either describe a relationship or show possession. They don't act alone—no solo careers for prepositions. Prepositions act as part of prepositional phrases.

Keep that secret <u>between you and me</u>.

Between describes where the secret is to be kept. If I said "I'll tell you the secret at dinnertime," *at dinnertime* is the prepositional phrase, and *at* describes when the secret will be revealed.

1-35

CONJUNCTIONS: AND THE WINNER IS . . .

Sometimes you have so much to say that you can just go on and on. What connects your thoughts? Conjunctions.

A **conjunction** connects words, phrases, and parts of sentences. Common conjunctions are *and, but*, and *or*.

There is more to conjunctions than what we'll deal with here. We'll save the more complicated uses for later when we talk about creating sentences and using punctuation. For now, let's focus on the simple conjunctions.

1-36

COORDINATING CONJUNCTIONS

I like to think of **coordinating conjunctions** as organizing (or coordinating) the sentence or phrase—sort of like a fashion stylist choosing pieces to coordinate the right outfit, or a coach with a whistle coordinating team members for a play.

Coordinating conjunctions are the FANBOYS of language. They all have fewer than four letters.

For
And
Nor
But
Or
Yet
So

Putting Coordinating Conjunctions to Work

To help build a sentence, conjunctions join other words, phrases, or clauses that have the same construction. You'll get what I mean by "the same construction" in the examples below.

> Squiggly was often distracted by this or that.
> (*This* and *that* are both single pronouns.)

> Squiggly went to the store and bought some chocolate.
> (*Went to the store* and *bought some chocolate* are both verb phrases.)

> Squiggly went to the store, and Aardvark wondered when he would return.
> (*Squiggly went to the store* and *Aardvark wondered when he would return* are both clauses or sentences that could stand on their own. You'll learn more about clauses in section 2-4.)

Note that an entire clause (including a verb) can follow a conjunction.

Parallel Construction and Conjunctions

In every example above, a coordinating conjunction properly joined similar parts of a sentence. This is called **parallel construction**. Parallel construction is even used in simple lists.

> Aardvark bought a tie, shirt, and a hat for Squiggly.
> (wrong because the list items are different.)

> Aardvark bought a tie, a shirt, and a hat for Squiggly.
> (right because each list item is a noun with an article.)

> Squiggly wishes for a bicycle, the tent, and for a kite.
> (so wrong!)

> Squiggly wishes for a bicycle, for a tent, and for a kite.
> (right)

Squiggly wishes for <u>a</u> bicycle, <u>a</u> tent, and <u>a</u> kite.
(right)

Squiggly wishes for a bicycle, tent, and kite.
(right)

BEWARE

Don't overuse the words *and* and *or*. It will exhaust your reader.

> Squiggly picked Grammar Girl and Aardvark and Harry and Sally and Anna and Charlie.

That has too many *and*s. Instead, use commas.

> Squiggly picked Grammar Girl, Aardvark, Harry, Sally, Anna, and Charlie.

1-37

CORRELATIVE CONJUNCTIONS

Certain conjunctions are codependent; they don't like being alone, so they combine with other words to form **correlative conjunctions** such as the following:

both . . . and	neither . . . nor
either . . . or	not only . . . but also

> "<u>Either</u> be friends with Aardvark <u>or</u> I'm not playing," Grammar Girl insisted.

> Now <u>neither</u> Grammar Girl <u>nor</u> Aardvark is on Squiggly's team.

> Aardvark is <u>not only</u> a great player <u>but also</u> a great negotiator.

POP QUIZ

Fill in the blanks.

1. He had _____ 3.8 grade point average.
   a or **an**

2. Grammar Girl was excited that her picture was in
   _____ sports section of the local newspaper.
   a or **the**

3. Squiggly _____ hopped _____ skipped;
   neither or **either**   **nor** or **or**

   he just walked slowly.

4. Aardvark liked _____ ketchup _____
   not only or **either**   **but also** or **and**

   mustard.

SUBORDINATING CONJUNCTIONS

1-38

At a job, your subordinates are the people who work for you, the people who are under you on the organizational chart. In grammar, **subordinate clauses** work for the main clause in a sentence. They can't stand alone. Subordinate clauses are headed by subordinating conjunctions such as *because, before, if, since, though, when, whenever,* and *while*.

> Aardvark left the room <u>whenever</u> Squiggly turned on polka music.

> Squiggly warned Aardvark <u>before</u> he turned on the music.

You'll learn more about how to use subordinating conjunctions in the Phrases and Clauses section of the next chapter (section 2-4).

INTERJECTIONS

<u>Yo</u>! Do you know what an interjection is?

<u>Um</u>, not really.

<u>Wow</u>!

<u>Yes</u>, you have a problem with that?

<u>Well</u>, how can you say you don't know what an interjection is?

As you can see, interjections (the underlined words above) are short words or phrases that reveal emotions, offer reactions, insert pauses, and demand attention. They are also sometimes called **exclamations.**

Sometimes they are at the beginning of a sentence. Sometimes they stand alone as a one-word sentence.

Chapter Two

Sentenced for Life

G REAT! YOU HAVE your parts of speech—the batteries of grammar. It's time to use them to light up your world, to give voice to your thoughts, and to make sure others know or understand how you think.

It's time to create sentences.

Unfortunately, you can't turn any set of words into a sentence by just starting with a capital letter and ending with a period.

By the basic definition, a sentence has a subject and a predicate. (Although it is a bit simplistic, it can help to think of the predicate as the verb for now.)

Here's an example of a very simple sentence with just a subject and a verb:

Squiggly ran.

SUBJECTS

The **subject** is the one taking action. Subjects can take different forms.

The simplest subject is a single noun.

> Squiggly ran.

If you have two or more nouns, you have a **compound subject** when they're joined by *and*, and an **alternative subject** when they're joined by *or*.

> Squiggly and Aardvark ran. (compound subject)
> Squiggly or Aardvark called. (alternative subject)

Do you remember gerunds from section 1-9? They are verbs that are turned into nouns by adding *ing* to the end. They can also act as the subject of a sentence:

> Singing makes me happy. (gerund as subject)

A verbal form called an infinitive (section 1-11) can also act as the subject of a sentence:

> To laugh is to live. (infinitive as subject)
> To err is human; to forgive is divine.

Phrases are groups of words that work together in a sentence but are missing a subject, a predicate, or both. A phrase is like a clause (see below) that lost some of its parts. One example is a noun phrase. The reason I'm telling you this is that a noun phrase can act as the subject of a sentence. When it does, it's called the **complete subject**, and the noun nugget it contains is called the **simple subject**. In this sentence the complete subject is in italics and the simple subject is underlined:

> *The friendly yellow snail* ran.

Clauses are groups of words that have a subject and predicate (verb). Sometimes a clause can be the subject of a sentence. For example, a quotation or book title can be the subject of a sentence:

> *She Sang Weakly* is more than 200 pages.

> "You must leave" meant something. (If this is confusing, think of the sentence in a larger story. "You must leave" could be a note Squiggly found scratched on the door.)

As with phrases, when a clause is the subject, you can talk about the complete subject (the whole clause) or the simple subject (the bare-bones subject). Note that when any clause acts like a noun (for example, serving as a subject), it can be called a **noun clause**.

> What he says in his sleep makes us wonder about his dreams.
> How we will explain ourselves is open to debate.

A sentence that doesn't seem to have a subject usually has an implied subject. For example, in this imperative sentence (see section 1-7), the implied subject is *you*:

> Run!

PREDICATES

2-2

The **predicate** is the part of the sentence that isn't the subject. A sentence must have a verb, and in a very simple sentence, the predicate is the verb. For example, in the following sentence, *Squiggly* is the subject and *ran* is the predicate:

> Squiggly ran.

The predicate can include things that modify the verb, such as objects and adverbs. For example, if an adverb such as *quickly* modifies the verb, it is part of the predicate.

Squiggly <u>ran quickly</u>.

If your sentence has a linking verb (see section 1-5), such as *is*, the element that comes after it is called a **predicate noun** when it is a noun and a **predicate adjective** when it is an adjective. In these two examples, the predicate is underlined, and the predicate noun and predicate adjective are in italics:

The ring <u>is *a doozy*</u>. (predicate noun)
Silence <u>is *golden*</u>. (predicate adjective)

2-3 DIRECT AND INDIRECT OBJECTS

If you remember our discussion of transitive and intransitive verbs from section 1-4, you'll know that some sentences need more than a subject and a verb. If you're dealing with a transitive verb—it transfers its action to an object—your sentence will also need an *object*. There are two kinds: *direct objects* and *indirect objects*.

A **direct object** is the direct recipient of the verb's action. In the sentences below, the transitive verb is underlined and the direct object is in italics.

Squiggly <u>bought</u> *rocks*. (***bought rocks*** is the predicate)

Aardvark <u>spelled</u> *the next word*. (***spelled the next word*** is the predicate)

An **indirect object** is needed when the direct object alone doesn't tell the story. The indirect object is the person or thing that receives the direct object.

In the sentences below, the transitive verb is underlined, the direct object is in italics, and the indirect object is capitalized:

Squiggly <u>gave</u> ME *rocks.* (*gave me rocks* is the predicate)

Aardvark <u>sent</u> HIS MOTHER *flowers.* (*sent his mother flowers* is the predicate)

She <u>threw</u> HIM *a kiss.* (*threw him a kiss* is the predicate)

Notice that you can't have an indirect object without a direct object.

POP QUIZ

Underline the predicate in each sentence.

1. Squiggly looked longingly at the chocolate.
2. The boy with blue hair called.
3. Sir Fragalot messed up his sentence again.

Answers: 1. looked longingly at the chocolate; 2. called; 3. messed up his sentence again

---

PHRASES AND CLAUSES

2-4

Phrases and clauses are both groups of words that work together in a sentence. A clause has a subject and predicate, and a phrase is missing something.

You already learned that a noun phrase can act as the subject of a sentence (see section 2-1). Phrases are quite flexible and can act as almost any part of a sentence or part of speech. Here are some examples of phrases:

The house that Jack built stood on the hill.
(noun phrase)

We should have gone to the store.
(verb phrase)

The teacher of the month claimed her award.
(prepositional phrase)

To remember soldiers' service is to honor their sacrifice.
(infinitive phrase)

Swimming upstream, the salmon would soon spawn.
(gerund phrase)

Trees grown without love will bear no fruit.
(participial phrase)

His tires changed, he reentered the race.
(absolute phrase)

If a clause can stand on its own as a sentence, it is called a **main clause** or an **independent clause**.

Santa Claus rides a sleigh.

If a clause can't stand on its own as a sentence, it's called a **dependent clause** or a **subordinate clause**. Dependent clauses are headed by words called **subordinating conjunctions** such as *since* and *because* (see section 1-38). A dependent clause needs a main clause to ground it. If it's left all alone, it's considered a sentence fragment (see sidebar box in section 2-6). In the sentences below, the dependent clauses are underlined:

Santa makes good time because he rides a sleigh.
Since Santa Claus finds another way in when there isn't a chimney, he can still visit kids who live in apartments.

TYPES OF SENTENCES, PART I

Sentences come in four flavors: declarative, exclamatory, interrogative, and imperative.

Declarative sentences make a statement. Scarlett O'Hara in *Gone with the Wind* says, "I do declare, I was surprised to see you turn out to be such a noble character." She says she's going to make a declaration and then she does: the declarative sentence *I was surprised to see you turn out to be such a noble character.*

Exclamatory sentences are just excited declarative sentences. They are statements that end with an exclamation point. *He stole my phone! I've told him a thousand times not to go into my room!*

Interrogative sentences ask a question. When you are interrogating someone, you ask a lot of questions. Think of interrogative sentences as part of the interrogation. *Where were you? Why were you late? Did you try to call?*

Imperative sentences make commands or requests, and the subject is missing or, more accurately, is implied to be *you*. *Run! Come home. Get out.*

TYPES OF SENTENCES, PART II

You knew that when there was a Types of Sentences, Part I, title, I'd get to Part II. Sentences can be sliced and diced another way: into categories called simple, compound, complex, and compound-complex sentences.

Simple sentences are what they sound like: simple. They have only one main clause.

Squiggly ran.
The tall, hairy bear scared the inexperienced campers.

Compound sentences are made by joining main clauses.

Squiggly ran, and Aardvark stood his ground.
(MAIN CLAUSE)   (MAIN CLAUSE)

The bear scared the campers; he was tall and hairy.
(MAIN CLAUSE)   (MAIN CLAUSE)

Complex sentences have at least one main clause and one dependent clause.

If Santa makes all the toys, the elves won't have enough work.
(DEPENDENT CLAUSE)   (MAIN CLAUSE)

I want cheesecake because it is my birthday.
(MAIN CLAUSE)   (DEPENDENT CLAUSE)

You may think you know what compound-complex sentences are at this point, but bear with me because it's not the obvious choice. **Compound-complex sentences** are formed when you have at least two main clauses and at least one dependent clause.

Squiggly got matches; Aardvark needed help with the fire
(MAIN CLAUSE)   (MAIN CLAUSE)
because he was afraid of the dark.
(DEPENDENT CLAUSE)

I had 20 friends over because it was my birthday, and
(MAIN CLAUSE)   (DEPENDENT CLAUSE)
I wanted everyone to have cheesecake.
(MAIN CLAUSE)

FRAGMENTED

Anything that isn't a sentence is a fragment.

Although fragments aren't evil, you'll mostly want to avoid them. (I will discuss them more in Chapter Five.) I have an easy three-step test to figure out whether you have a fragment or a sentence.

1. The easiest test is to ask yourself if there is a verb. If there's no verb, then it's probably a fragment.
2. If there is just one word, ask yourself if the sentence is an exclamation or an interjection (Wow!) or a command (Go!). If it's not, then it's a fragment.
3. If it has a subject and verb, ask yourself if it is complete. If it isn't complete, it is a fragment (otherwise known as a dependent clause). This last step is a little trickier, but I'm sure you can do it!

POP QUIZ

Which of the following is *not* a fragment?

1. The cat with nine lives.
2. Super!
3. Although he fell 20 feet.

Answer: 2

SUBJECT-VERB AGREEMENT: CAN'T WE ALL JUST GET ALONG ?

Singular nouns take singular verbs, and plural nouns take plural verbs. It's really quite simple.

> I am happy.
> We are happy.
> She runs.
> They run.

Note that verbs are not like nouns; you don't add *s* to make them plural.

Easy, yes? But wait! Some tricky situations might cause you to doubt yourself.

CONJUNCTIONS AND AGREEMENT

2-8

The conjunction *and* adds things together. So when you see the word *and* between two subjects, the verb is *usually* plural (see the box below for examples of some exceptions). In the following sentence, the subject—*Squiggly and Aardvark*—is plural, so the verb is plural:

> <u>Squiggly and Aardvark</u> are eating ice cream.

Remember, you learned at the beginning of this chapter (section 2-1) that this is called a compound subject.

When *or* or *nor* is used as the conjunction, the rule gets trickier, but it's consistent. *Or* doesn't add anything together—it's one or the other. So if each item is singular in your alternative subject, then the verb is singular.

> <u>Squiggly or Aardvark</u> is eating ice cream.

If each part of your alternative subject is plural, the verb is plural.

The aunts or the uncles are eating ice cream.

If one part of your alternative subject is singular and the other part is plural, make your verb match the part that is closest to it.

Squiggly or the aunts are eating.
The uncles or Aardvark is eating.

I repeat: the verb agrees with the subject that is closest to the verb (or the second subject, if that is easier for you to remember). Tricky perhaps, but there are no exceptions!

Some style guides recommend always putting the plural subject last in sentences such as these (except when *I* is one of the subjects; *I* always goes last—see section 2-12).

Except That . . .

1. Objects that usually go together may be considered singular, such as peanut butter and jelly, ham and eggs, and milk and cookies.

   Milk and cookies is my favorite snack.

2. When the amount is thought of as one complete whole, use a singular verb.

   Two hundred dollars is a lot to spend for a pair of shoes.
   Three miles is far.

3. Some words end in s but they are singular—examples include *news*, *mathematics*, *rabies*, and *billiards*.

   The news makes her happy.

4. Look up tricky words in the dictionary to see which are plural and which are singular. For instance, *phenomena* is plural. *Phenomenon* is singular.

INDEFINITE PRONOUNS: PRONOUN PANDEMONIUM

Remember indefinite pronouns? Instead of referring to a specific person such as *he* or *she*, **indefinite pronouns** refer to vague (indefinite) people or things, and figuring out whether they are singular or plural can be tricky. For example, the indefinite pronoun *everyone* sounds like a lot of people, but in grammar land, *everyone* is a singular noun and takes a singular verb:

> Everyone is happy. (right)
> Everyone are happy. (wrong)

Everyone and *everybody* mean the same thing and are interchangeable, so *everybody* takes a singular verb too. The same rules hold true for *anyone* and *anybody*, and *no one* and *nobody*—they're singular and interchangeable. Pronouns beginning with *any* (*anyone, anybody, anything*), *every* (*everyone, everybody, everything*), *no* (*no one, nobody, nothing*), and *some* (*someone, somebody, something*) are singular.

There are also indefinite pronouns that are always plural, such as *both, few, several,* and *many.* They need plural verbs.

> Both are happy. (right)
> Both is happy. (wrong)

And then there are those indefinite pronouns that can't make up their minds. The sentence has to tell you whether the pronoun is plural or singular.

> Most of the sisters are redheads.

(*Sisters* is plural and that is what *most* is representing.)

> Most of her hair is dyed red.

(*Hair* is singular and that is what *most* is representing.)

> Twelve boys played, and none are tired.

(*None* is a way of saying *not any.*)

> Of all the lessons, none is more important than this.

(*None* is a way of saying *not one.*)

Indefinite Pronouns

Some indefinite pronouns are always singular, some are always plural, and some can be singular or plural depending on the sentence. These are some examples of each type:

Singular		Plural	Singular or Plural
another	little	both	all
anybody	much	few	any
anyone	neither	many	more
each	nobody	others	most
either	no one	several	none
everybody	somebody		some
everyone	someone		

2-10 COLLECTIVE NOUNS: LET'S TAKE UP A COLLECTION

Collective nouns are words such as *team*, *family*, *orchestra*, and *band*; they are nouns that describe a group. Again, they sound like a lot of people, but they are usually singular nouns.

The family is going on vacation next week.
The orchestra plays on Thursdays.
The board of directors meets monthly.

I have another example from *Star Trek*. To remember that collective nouns are usually singular, think of the Borg. (For the uninitiated, the Borg is a group of cyborgs who don't have a sense of individuality, and they call themselves a "collective.") With the Borg, the collective acts as one—singular. In grammar, collective nouns are usually singular.

There's an exception, though: Some collective nouns, such as *couple*, are considered plural if each person has a sense of individuality. (I know that is terribly vague, but it's the rule.)

For example, you would say "The couple are vacationing separately this year" because there is a sense that it is two individual people doing two separate things. But you would say "Each couple is going to Bermuda on a different week" because each pair is being spoken of as a unit. You just have to use your best judgment, and even though this seems tricky, the good news is that you can never really get it wrong because you can always say that you were thinking of the couple as individuals (or a unit) if someone questions your verb choice.

What's UP with That?

Band names (and company names) are generally singular in the United States, but some people go by the rule that if the name sounds plural (like The Beatles and Black Eyed Peas), they treat it as plural, and if it sounds singular (like Lifehouse or Coldplay), they treat it as singular. On the other hand, team names are often treated as plural even if they sound singular. Don't worry about it too much; simply be consistent or follow your teacher's preference.

TRICKY SITUATIONS

Sometimes our writing and thoughts are more complicated than a simple statement like *Everyone is happy.*

What happens when your subject is singular, but the stuff on the other side of the verb is plural? Or your subject is plural but the phrase or clause on the other side of the verb is singular? Which does the verb agree with?

The verb agrees with the subject. Don't be confused by what happens on the right side of the verb.

The biggest <u>pain</u> about camping <u>is</u> the mosquitoes.
(SUBJECT)   (VERB)

The two <u>boys</u> <u>prefer</u> the roller coaster.
(SUBJECT) (VERB)

What happens when a preposition gets between your subject and verb? Believe me, it can happen. Prepositional phrases can act as adjectives (describing which one) or adverbs (describing how, when, or where).

All you need to create a prepositional phrase is a preposition (duh!) and a noun, pronoun, or gerund (with modifiers thrown in, if you want).

The <u>names on the cake</u> <u>were</u> Squiggly and Aardvark.
(SUBJECT)   ↑   (VERB)

(PREPOSITIONAL PHRASE)

Names is the subject. *On the cake* tells you where the names are (it's a prepositional phrase acting as an adverb), but the sentence is about the names, so the subject and verb are both plural.

What happens when your writing gets all tricky and the subject shows up at the end of a sentence? Again, make the verb agree with the subject.

On the ship <u>were</u> my <u>friends.</u>
(VERB)   (SUBJECT)

The subject isn't the *ship*. The subject is *friends*. They were on the ship. If you rewrite this sentence, you'll see the subject and the verb more clearly.

My <u>friends</u> <u>were</u> on the ship.
    (SUBJECT) (VERB)

POP QUIZ

Fill in the blanks.

1. Neither her parents nor her sister _____ her new friends.
   like or **likes**

2. A few of us _____ going to the game.
   are or **is**

3. The CDs on the shelf in the living room _____ too scratched.
   is or **are**

Answers: 1. likes; 2. are; 3. are

✓✓ Check It Out ✓✓

These phrases are out to confuse you. Use them in your sentences, but ignore them when figuring out subject-verb agreement. They are not functioning as conjunctions—they are not the same as *and*—so they don't make the subject plural.

accompanied by   as well as   including
along with   in addition to   together with

<u>Squiggly</u>, along with Aardvark, <u>sings</u> in the band.

<u>The whole class</u>, including Squiggly and Aardvark, <u>is</u> in the play. ✓

PRONOUNS AND AGREEMENT

You remember our hardworking pronouns that stand in for nouns, right? (See section 1-12.) Well, sometimes the noun and its stunt double are in the same sentence. (Nouns are egomaniacs, I tell you!) Just as in the movies where the stunt double must look like the star, the pronoun must look like the noun. In grammar talk, the pronoun must agree with the noun, which we call the **antecedent**. The word *antecedent* is similar to the word *ancestor*, and you can remember that just as a person "descends" from his or her ancestor, the pronoun descends from the noun.

It could be as simple a sentence as

> He is Squiggly.

He is the pronoun, and *Squiggly* (the noun) is the antecedent. Note that *he* is singular and male, like Squiggly.

> When Aardvark cried, her face turned red. (wrong)

Aardvark is not a she.

> When Aardvark cried, his face turned red. (right)

His refers to Aardvark.

> Aardvark and Squiggly ran so fast, we caused a breeze. (wrong)

We is first person plural, but the antecedent is third person plural.

> Aardvark and Squiggly ran so fast, they caused a breeze. (right)

Two nouns joined by *and* make a plural compound subject, and *they* is a plural pronoun.

QUICK AND DIRTY TIP

Pronouns and antecedents must agree in gender, number, and person.

The tricky part is when you have a few nouns. The pronoun should refer to the closest noun. Sometimes, when the pronouns are scattered, it's hard to know which noun the pronoun is connected to, and that's when you get sentences that are either confusing or funny (because of the confusion).

> Aardvark ate so much cake that his stomach hurt. <u>It</u> was covered with chocolate frosting, and <u>it</u> felt like <u>it</u> was going to explode. (wrong)

No matter how much cake you eat, your stomach isn't going to be covered in frosting, nor will the cake explode. The writer means for the first *it* to refer to cake, but because of the way *it* follows *his*

stomach, it is actually referring to his stomach. Ridiculous! His stomach isn't covered with chocolate frosting. The antecedent to the first *it* should be *cake*, but it's too far away to be sure. The writer means for the second *it* to refer to *stomach*, but again, its placement makes the sentence confusing. Avoid using the same pronoun (*it*, in this case) to refer to two different nouns.

Rewriting is the way to fix these sentences.

> Aardvark ate so much of the chocolate-frosted cake that he thought his stomach would explode. (right)

OR

> Aardvark ate so much of the chocolate-frosted cake that his stomach hurt. It felt like it was going to explode. (right)

Note how in this sentence *it* directly follows its antecedent—*his stomach*—as it should.

Be Polite when Ordering Nouns and Pronouns . . . in a Sentence

It's a matter of politeness, not grammar, that leads people to put themselves last in a list. In the same way that you hold a door open to let others walk through first, you should let everyone else go before you in your sentences.

> Squiggly and I went to Aardvark's party.
> Aardvark gave Squiggly and me party favors.

Even when you're using the possessive pronoun *my*, you put yourself last in the list.

> Squiggly's and my gift made Aardvark very happy.

On the other hand, all pronouns besides *I* and *me* normally come before nouns. Crazy world, huh? The following sentences are correct.

You and Squiggly are invited to the party.

She and Squiggly went to Aardvark's party.

Aardvark gave her and Squiggly party favors.

Aardvark, Squiggly, and I are happy that you're reading this book.

We're happy and grammatically correct!

POP QUIZ

Choose the best sentence for each:

1. A. Him and Sue come over every Sunday.
   B. Sue and him come over every Sunday.
   C. He and Sue come over every Sunday.
   D. Sue and he come over every Sunday.

2. A. They like to visit Pat's and my house.
   B. They like to visit Pat's and me house.
   C. They like to visit me and Pat's house.
   D. They like to visit my and Pat's house.

Answers: 1. C; 2. A

CREATING SENTENCES

2-13

Now that we have the basics of sentence structure down, let's focus on the different ways to begin a sentence. We'll start with individual words—the good and the not-so-good ones. Then we'll get into phrases and clauses. After that we'll tackle those phrases and clauses that come in the middle of sentences.

THE FANBOYS ARE BACK

Remember coordinating conjunctions, otherwise known as the FANBOYS (see section 1-36)? Should you start a sentence with one of them? That's a tough question.

By now you've probably figured out that I tend to be on the relaxed side of the language divide, and relaxed people think it's OK to start a sentence with a coordinating conjunction like *and*, *but*, and *or*. Actually, most sticklers think it's OK too. It's a matter of style and formality. Starting a sentence with a coordinating conjunction is an informal style; it makes your writing sound conversational. You just need to determine whether formality or informality is appropriate.

In addition, a conjunction at the beginning usually draws attention to the sentence and adds punch.

> I couldn't find the answer in my library. And I have a lot of books.

And highlights the fact that even with all my books, I couldn't find the answer.

The punch is one of the reasons you don't want to overdo starting sentences with the FANBOYS—you want to pick and choose what you emphasize. You don't want to sock your reader over the head with all your points. Look at what happens when coordinating conjunctions are overused:

> I couldn't find the answer in my library. And I have a lot of books. Yet my books are old. But they're very valuable. And my library takes up two rooms. Or is it three rooms?

The above is correct, but I think I would want to scream after the second sentence.

The other problem is that if you don't use the FANBOYS correctly, you can create sentence fragments.

And looking for the answer. (wrong)

But hanging out at the beach. (wrong)

The examples above have no subjects. They are fragments.

Most school papers demand formal writing unless they're creative writing assignments. Generally, teachers don't say "Give me an essay about the Constitution by Friday, and make sure it's written in an informal style." So, be cautious about starting sentences with the FANBOYS.

STARTING A SENTENCE WITH *BECAUSE* (AND OTHER SUBORDINATING CONJUNCTIONS)

2-15

Subordinating conjunctions join subordinate—or dependent—clauses to other clauses (See section 1-38). A subordinate clause can help make your writing more interesting, but this is another tricky area because it's easy to create fragments with subordinating conjunctions.

Because is one of the subordinating conjunctions. When a subordinating conjunction begins a clause, it makes that clause dependent on (or subordinate to) a main clause.

When you start a sentence with one of these critters, make sure you have a main clause to go with it.

> Some people mistakenly believe that you can't start a sentence with a subordinating conjunction. So wrong! It's completely allowed—you just have to make sure you attach a main clause to it.

Because Aardvark wanted to go fishing. (wrong)

When we get back from vacation. (wrong)

These are fragments, not sentences. They are missing a main clause.

As long as you include the main clause later in the sentence, subordinating conjunctions like *because*, *when*, and *unless* are acceptable sentence starters.

> Because Aardvark wanted to go fishing, we had to get up at four in the morning.

> When we get home from vacation, I'm going to buckle down at school.

The main clause explains the subordinated part. Suddenly, it's not a sentence fragment; it's a complex sentence with a main clause and a dependent clause led by a subordinating conjunction.

Truthfully, you can usually reverse the clauses to avoid starting the sentence with *because* and its friends, but you shouldn't have to. No grammatical rule exists to stand in your way.

> We had to get up at four in the morning because Aardvark wanted to go fishing.

> I'm going to buckle down at school when we get home from vacation.

(Wondering if you need a comma? No worries! We'll deal with punctuation in the next chapter.)

COMMON SUBORDINATING CONJUNCTIONS		
after	how	that
although	if	though
as	lest	unless
as if	now that	until
as in	once	when
as long as	provided	whenever
because	rather than	where
before	since	whereas
despite	so that	whether
even though	than	while

SENTENCE ADVERBS

Adverbs can describe whole sentences. When they do this, they are called (unimaginatively) sentence adverbs. Remember how I said adverbs, with the word *verb* in their name, are superactive? Here they go again! Adverbs are obviously workaholics, describing almost everything, including sentences.

Common Sentence Adverbs

Sentence adverbs are words that modify a whole sentence. Examples of sentence adverbs include the following:

clearly	ironically
fortunately	mercifully
frankly	remarkably
happily	thankfully
honestly	unfortunately

Here are some examples of sentence adverbs in action:

Fortunately, the skunks were upwind.

Honestly, I wish I were somewhere else.

I am hopeful that you can see that the sentence adverbs *fortunately* and *honestly* modify the *whole* sentence. *Fortunately* relates to the entire point that the skunks were upwind, and *honestly* describes the subject's state of mind and gives the whole sentence a confessional quality.

Some people believe the word *hopefully* is a sentence adverb just like *fortunately* and *honestly*, but other people believe *hopefully* can be only an adverb that describes verbs, as in *Squiggly stared hopefully at the chocolate*. They don't believe it can mean "I am hopeful that...." Because of these two different points of view, starting a sentence with *hopefully* is controversial. Believe it or not, people get really worked up about this kind of stuff.

There are instances where your meaning wouldn't be clear if you started a sentence with *hopefully*. For example, in the following sentence, did Squiggly pick up some chocolate with a hopeful disposition, or is someone hopeful that Squiggly picked up some chocolate?

> Hopefully, Squiggly picked up some chocolate.

I don't believe, however, that there are many instances where a reasonable person would be confused because the context (the surrounding words) usually makes the meaning clear. In the following sentences it is clear the *writer* is hopeful, not the book, the weather, or Aardvark.

> Hopefully, the book will do well.
> Hopefully, it won't rain.
> We don't have chips to go with the salsa. Hopefully,
> Aardvark is getting chips on his way home.

Frankly, even though I believe *hopefully* does function as a sentence adverb at the beginning of sentences, I still can't use it that way. People get too upset.

If you believe *hopefully* is a sentence adverb and you don't care what people think of you, you can start a sentence with *hopefully*. If you want to be safe, substitute *I am hopeful that* for *hopefully* at the beginning of sentences. (How's that for putting all the responsibility on you?)

You might be wondering whether it is OK to start a sentence with the word *however*. We need to talk about some other things first, but if you can't wait, see that entry in Chapter Four.

ORDERING YOUR SENTENCES AROUND

You are the boss of your sentences. You decide how they are set up. The subject doesn't have to be at the beginning of the sentence.

Simple sentences are straightforward. It's hard to get confused with this sentence:

(SUBJECT) (VERB)

As you know from reading and from your own writing, many sentences aren't that basic. If they were all that short, readers would be catching z's in no time.

That is why grammarians invented clauses and phrases that can act as modifiers. OK, maybe they didn't invent these parts of sentences, but they sure have a lot to say about them.

MISPLACED MODIFIERS: LOCATION, LOCATION, LOCATION

Modifiers are just what they sound like—words or phrases that modify or specify or describe something else (see section 1-23). Where you place modifying phrases or words determines whether you have a sentence of beauty or one that should work in a comedy club.

Misplaced modifiers attach themselves to something you didn't intend them to describe. We'll start with simple modifier errors and work our way to the more complex squinting modifiers.

Again with the grammar excitement!

Simple Misplaced Modifiers

Even one itty-bitty word in the wrong place can be confusing. (Of course, they're also fun because they can create all sorts of silly misunderstandings. Grammar Girl is easily amused.)

For example, the word *only* is a simple modifier that's easy to misplace.

These two sentences mean different things:

Squiggly ate <u>only chocolate</u>.
Squiggly <u>only ate</u> chocolate.

The first sentence (*Squiggly ate only chocolate*) means that Squiggly ate nothing but chocolate—no fruit, no meat, just chocolate.

The second sentence (*Squiggly only ate chocolate*) means that all Squiggly did with chocolate was eat it. He didn't buy, melt, or sell it. He only ate it.

When you're working with one-word modifiers, such as *only*, they usually go right before the word they modify.

Here's another example of two sentences with very different meanings:

Aardvark <u>almost failed</u> every art class he took.
Aardvark failed <u>almost every</u> art class he took.

The first sentence (*Aardvark almost failed every art class he took*) means that although it was close, he passed all those classes.

The second sentence (*Aardvark failed almost every art class he took*) means that he passed a few art classes.

Note again that the modifier *almost* acts on what directly follows it: *almost failed* versus *almost every art class*. In either case, Aardvark is probably not going to make a living as a painter, but these two sentences mean different things.

Check It Out

One-word modifiers should usually go right before the word they modify. ✓

Misplaced Participial Phrases

You've seen how one misplaced word can change the meaning of your sentence. Now see what a misplaced phrase can do.

Remember, a participle is a verb that acts like an adjective when *ing*, *ed*, or *en* is added to the end, unless the verb is irregular. Participles of irregular verbs can have different endings. (See section 1-10.) A **participial phrase** includes modifiers or objects. It can be at the beginning or middle of a sentence. It's also known as a modifying phrase.

The word *participial* reminds me of *marsupial* (my mind can be a scary place), so I imagine phrases tucked in a kangaroo's pouch that are pulled out to add interest to a sentence. Of course, a participial phrase describes the closest noun just as a simple modifier does.

> Filled with insecurities, the girl cried at every imagined hurt. (*Filled with insecurities* describes the girl.)

Or the sentence could be written this way:

> The girl, filled with insecurities, cried at every imagined hurt.

Notice how in both sentences the participial phrase either came right before or right after the noun it was describing. When you have a phrase at the beginning of a sentence, the noun described should immediately follow the comma. (We'll cover commas in the next chapter—see section 3-5.)

Let's go back to my participial/marsupial image. (Yup, you have to.) Let's say the kangaroo goes wild, carelessly throwing phrases around. Look at what happens to the meaning of the sentence if the participial phrase is separated from the noun.

> Filled with insecurities, every imagined hurt made the girl cry. (wrong)

The girl's tears, <u>filled with insecurities</u>, reflected every imagined hurt. (wrong)

The first sentence means that the hurt was filled with insecurities. The second sentence is even more confusing—were her tears filled with insecurities?

Follow the simple rule that the modifying phrase goes directly before or after the thing it modifies. If not, you could end up with hysterically funny images just when you want your reader to take you seriously.

Here's another example of what not to do, which might better demonstrate the two different images:

<u>Covered in wildflowers</u>, Aardvark pondered the hillside's beauty.

In that sentence, Aardvark, not the hillside, is covered with wildflowers because the name *Aardvark* comes directly after the modifying phrase *covered in wildflowers*.

<u>Covered in wildflowers</u>, the hillside appeared beautiful to Aardvark.

Here the words *the hillside* immediately follow the modifying phrase *covered in wildflowers*. It now means that it's a wildflower-covered hill.

Or better yet, I could write *Aardvark pondered the beauty of the wildflowers that covered the hillside*.

I can think of even more ways to write the sentence, but the point is to be careful. Make sure the phrases are modifying what you intend.

POP QUIZ

Which sentence is most clear?

1. Afraid of what he would say, her heart beat quickly.
2. Her heart beat quickly, afraid of what he would say.
3. Afraid of what he would say, she felt her heart beat quickly.
4. Her heart, beats quickly, afraid of what he would say.

Answer: 3

Misplaced Prepositional Phrases

Prepositional phrases are my favorite type of modifier, but if you're careless with their placement, they can turn your wonderful thoughts into foolish babbling.

> <u>With curls in her hair</u>, Aardvark thought the actress looked young.

The placement of the prepositional phrase *with curls in her hair* makes the sentence read as though Aardvark had curls in her hair. It's wrong on two counts: Aardvark is not a she, and it is the actress who has curls in her hair.

The sentence would be better written in the following way because *in her hair* describes where the curls are and *with curls* describes which actress.

> Aardvark thought the actress <u>with curls in her hair</u> looked young.

> OR

> <u>With curls in her hair</u>, the actress looked young—at least to Aardvark.

QUICK AND DIRTY TIP

To cut down on confusion, remember that modifiers, whether they are phrases or only one word, should be as close as possible to the word or phrase they are describing.

Dangling Modifiers: It's a Dangler

A **dangling modifier** describes something that isn't even in your sentence. Usually you are implying the subject and taking for granted that your reader will know what you mean—not a good strategy. Here's an example:

> <u>Hiking the trail</u>, the birds chirped loudly.

The way the sentence is written, the birds are hiking the trail because they are the only subject present. If that's not what you mean, you need to rewrite the sentence to something like this:

> Hiking the trail, Squiggly and Aardvark heard birds chirping loudly.

Squinting Modifiers: Sun in Your Eyes?

How do you make a modifier squint? By placing it between two things that it could reasonably modify, leaving the reader with no idea which one to choose.

> The boys who were running clumsily jumped aside.

As written, that sentence could mean two different things: clumsily running boys jumped aside or running boys jumped aside clumsily.

In the original sentence (*The boys who were running clumsily jumped aside*), the word *clumsily* is squinting between the words *running* and *jumped*. I think "shifty modifier" would be a better name, but I don't get to name these things (yet).

So remember to be careful when using modifiers; they are easily misplaced, dangled, and made to squint.

While We're Talking About Location . . .

Avoid starting a sentence with a number if you can, but if you have to contort your writing, just write out the number and get on with your work. Unless you enjoy torturing your readers, it's usually worth the effort to rewrite the sentence when you're working with long or complex numbers. Consider, in these examples, how much easier the second sentence is to read:

> Twelve thousand eight hundred forty-two people attended the parade.

> The parade was attended by 12,842 people.

The second sentence uses the passive voice (see Chapter Five), but passive voice is better than writing out a humongous number and taking the risk that your readers' brains will be numb by the time they get to the verb.

Some style guides say it is OK to start a sentence with a numeral when it is a year or a proper name (for example, the company name 3M), but more stringent style guides say to rewrite the sentence. I think it is acceptable to start a sentence with a numeral in such cases, but use your own judgment—a formal audience may disagree.

1985 was a fabulous year. (questionable)
Everyone agreed that 1985 was a fabulous year. (better)

2-19

PARENTHETICAL EXPRESSIONS

Parenthetical expressions are phrases that are not necessary to the sentence but give extra information. These asides add flavor, a tidbit of information, or an extra thought. They work as commentaries. Without the parenthetical expression, the sentence would still be complete.

Aardvark, <u>as you can see for yourself</u>, is a snappy dresser.

Running away from home, <u>while never a good idea</u>, was definitely a mistake in the middle of a blizzard.

They're called parenthetical expressions because they could go in parentheses—but they don't have to. They could also be contained in commas or dashes. (We'll cover punctuation in Chapter Three.)

Appositives

Appositives are usually considered a special kind of parenthetical element. An appositive is a noun or noun phrase that is placed next to another noun or noun phrase to help identify it or to give more specific information. *Appositive* comes from the same root word as *apposition*, which means "the placing near or next to something." To remember the name, think of a soldier taking up a position next to the noun. Get it? *A position* equals *appositive*.

Appositives can be essential information or extra information. As always, place this phrase or noun right next to the noun it's describing.

> Thea, <u>the youngest of my sisters</u>, wishes she could live in Alaska.

> The girl with the ragged backpack, <u>Thea</u>, wished she could live in Alaska.

Essentially, What Is Essential?

It's time for a serious moment to ponder what is essential and what is not. Understanding this concept will help you determine whether you need punctuation, which words to use, and how to write exactly what you mean.

Sentences may contain **restrictive elements** and **nonrestrictive elements**. This means essential elements and nonessential elements.

Very simply put, a restrictive element is part of a sentence that you can't get rid of because it identifies the noun (or clause) specifically so the noun can't be confused with anything else.

> Any desserts <u>that contain chocolate</u> please Grammar Girl.

The words *that contain chocolate* restrict the kind of desserts you're talking about. Without them, the meaning of the sentence would change. Without them, you would be saying that all desserts please Grammar Girl, not just the ones with chocolate.

His friend <u>Squiggly</u> went to the store.

The name *Squiggly* identifies specifically which of his friends went to the store. *Squiggly*, in this sentence, is an essential (or restrictive) appositive.

A nonrestrictive element is something that can be left off without changing the meaning of the sentence. Think of a nonrestrictive element as simply additional information.

Diamonds, <u>which are expensive</u>, are the most common stones used in wedding rings.

His best friend, <u>Squiggly</u>, went to the store.

In Grammar Girl's world, all diamonds are expensive, so leaving out the words *which are expensive* doesn't change the meaning of the sentence.

Best friend, although perhaps changing from day to day, usually means one specific person. Anyone who knows the speaker in the second sentence already knows that Squiggly is the best friend, so *Squiggly* is a nonessential appositive (or the nonrestrictive element).

The commas, which we will discuss in the next chapter, help you recognize what is essential and what is not. The words *which* and *that* also specify whether the element is restrictive or nonrestrictive. (Check out *That* Versus *Which* in Chapter Four.)

Chapter Three

Punch Up Your Punctuation

YOU'VE BRUSHED UP on your grammar, you know what a sentence is, and you're daring anyone to stop you from ending a sentence with a preposition. Now all you need is punctuation.

Punctuation may seem like stupid little hacks and splashes on the page, but those marks actually help readers stay on track. Punctuation is a polite gesture: *Here, dear reader, allow me to guide you through this sentence. It's a long one, and it may be a little confusing, but I've provided clues and signposts along the way. I promise you won't get lost.*

We're going to start out easy with the period and work our way to the more exotic punctuation marks such as ellipses and asterisks. Finally, I make a solemn vow that you will conquer the dreaded apostrophe—the punctuation mark whose frequent misuse keeps language lovers in a nearly constant state of frustration (when they aren't waxing sentimental about the semicolon).

Grammar Girl must sit down from all the excitement!

TERMINAL PUNCTUATION: THE BEGINNING OF THE END

It might be a crazy place to begin, but we're starting with the ending, or terminal, punctuation marks—the marks you place at the end of a sentence.

PERIODS: SOMEBODY STOP ME!

The period is quite a straightforward punctuation mark. Everyone knows a period ends a sentence that is a statement, but the period—unlike the other final punctuation marks—can do more than just mark the end of a sentence.

Abbreviation Information

Any shortened form of a word is an abbreviation, for example, *ave.* for *avenue* and *Oct.* for *October.*

Some abbreviations are more commonly used than the actual words, such as *Mr.* for *mister, Mrs.* for *mistress*, and *etc.* for *et cetera.*

When you have an abbreviation at the end of a sentence, don't use a second period.

> Squiggly bought supplies for the trip—suntan lotion, a hat, a beach umbrella, a towel, etc.. (wrong)

> Squiggly bought supplies for the trip—suntan lotion, a hat, a beach umbrella, a towel, etc. (right)

The period at the end of the abbreviation becomes a superperiod (not the technical term) that does the task of both indicating the abbreviation and ending the sentence. (If you think losing the clear ending to a sentence will confuse your readers, rewrite the sentence so that the abbreviation doesn't come at the end, or write out the full word instead of using the abbreviation.)

On the other hand, when you end a question or an exclamation with an abbreviation, you do include both the period for the abbreviation and the final question mark or exclamation point.

Did Squiggly actually buy suntan lotion, a hat, a beach umbrella, a towel, etc.?

Acro-nymo-batics

Acronyms are a special kind of abbreviation. All acronyms are abbreviations, but not all abbreviations are acronyms.

Acronyms are made from the first letter (or letters) of a string of words but are pronounced as if they are words themselves. Examples include *NASA* (National Aeronautics and Space Administration), *NIMBY* (not in my backyard), and *ROFL* (rolling on the floor laughing).

Some acronyms have become such accepted words that they are written with lowercase letters, and many people don't even realize that they are acronyms: *scuba* (*s*elf-*c*ontained *u*nderwater *b*reathing *a*pparatus), *radar* (*ra*dio *d*etecting *a*nd *r*anging), and *laser* (*l*ight *a*mplification by *s*timulated *e*mission of *r*adiation).

No strict rule governs whether you should put periods after each letter in an acronym. Some publications put periods after each letter, arguing that because each letter is essentially an abbreviation for a word, periods are necessary. Other publications don't put periods after each letter, arguing that the copy looks cleaner without them, and because they are made of all capital letters, the fact that they are abbreviations is implied.

Once again, my advice is be consistent, or if your teacher asks for a specific style, follow that.

Squiggly always wanted to work for NASA.

Squiggly always wanted to work for N.A.S.A.

Initialisms are made from the first letter (or letters) of a string of words, but they don't make pronounceable words. *FBI* (Federal Bureau of Investigation), *FYI* (for your information), *PR* (public relations), and *CIA* (Central Intelligence Agency) are examples of initialisms. Go ahead, I dare you to pronounce CIA and FYI—nobody will know what you mean.

Initialisms are often confused with acronyms because they are made up of individual letters. Again, there is no strict rule for whether you should put periods after each letter in an initialism.

3-3

THE QUESTION MARK: HUH?

You think you already know how to ask questions? You do, don't you? I wonder if you're right. Should I believe you?

Everybody knows how to write a plain vanilla question, called a **direct question**.

> What's new?

But there are trickier scenarios. What happens when a sentence seems to be half statement, half question? What if you're asking an indirect question, asking a question that also seems to require an exclamation point, dealing with a quotation that contains a question, and so on?

So many questions. Luckily, Grammar Girl has the answers.

Questions Masquerading as Statements

Sometimes direct questions are tricky because they can look like statements, and the only way to tell your reader otherwise is to add a question mark. There's a big difference in meaning between these two sentences:

> Squiggly went to the store.
> Squiggly went to the store?

The question mark makes it a direct question that shows surprise. What the heck *was* Squiggly doing at the store?

Statements with Tag Questions

What about those little questions that come at the end of a statement?

> You didn't forget my birthday, did you?
> It's fun to play maracas, isn't it?

Bits like *did you* and *isn't it* are called **tag questions**, and they turn the whole sentence into a question, so use a question mark at the end.

> You do know, don't you, what to do if the tag is in the middle of the sentence?

Indirect Questions

Do you have a curious nature? Do you wonder about things?

When you wonder, your statements may sound like questions, but they're not direct questions, they're **indirect questions**, and they don't take a question mark.

> I wonder why he went to the store.

That's an indirect question—essentially a statement—so there's no question mark.

> Squiggly asked if fries came with his burger.

Again, it's not a question.

Indirect Questions Mixed with Direct Questions

It gets really crazy when you start mixing direct questions with other kinds of clauses. There are multiple ways to write something like *The question at hand is, who stole the cookies?* The simplest way to write that is to put a comma after the first clause and a question mark after the direct question, as I just did.

Believe it or not, some style guides allow you to capitalize the first word in a direct question even though it comes in the middle of a sentence: *The question at hand is, Who stole the cookies?* Supposedly, capitalizing the first word in the question places more emphasis on the question, but I think it makes the sentence look disjointed.

And if you think that looks weird, it gets even worse. If you flip the two parts around, you can put a question mark in the middle of your sentence: *Who stole the cookies? was the question at hand.*

It's good to know the rules, but these sentences seem so contorted that I believe it is better to try to rewrite them. I could easily convert the sentence to an indirect question.

Everyone wondered who stole the cookies.

Or I could use a colon (more on the colon later, in section 3-12) to make the punctuation less odd.

One question remained: who stole the cookies?

(See section 3-13 for a discussion of capitalizing the first letter after a colon.)

The Polite Question

Sometimes your sentence looks like a question, but it's merely being polite. If you're writing a polite command, you don't need a question mark.

Would you please let me do that for you.

Let It Snow: A Question Flurry

What if you have a bunch of questions and you want to string them all together?

> Can I have a cookie? two cookies? four cookies? twenty cookies?

Those add-on questions at the end aren't complete sentences, but each one gets a question mark anyway. Since they aren't complete sentences, you usually don't capitalize the first letter, but the rules are vague. Some guides say to capitalize the first letter if the questions are *nearly* a sentence or have sentence-like status, so you have to use your own judgment.

I don't consider *two cookies* nearly a sentence, but I may consider something like *two cookies and a squeaking ball to chase* nearly a sentence, which would make me consider capitalizing the first letter.

GET TO THE EXCLAMATION POINT

3-4

The exclamation point adds emphasis and indicates a strong emotion—surprise, panic, urgency, pain, horror. You get the picture.

> Don't overuse it! Stop now! Your writing will explode!

Don't overuse the exclamation point. If you do, your reader will stop believing that anything is as urgent as you claim. With the exclamation point, less is certainly more.

I'll have more to say about the exclamation point and the question mark when I discuss quotation marks later (see section 3-24).

We are leaving the punctuation that defines the ends of the sentences and delving into the guts of the sentence. Trust me, it isn't pretty.

COMMA COMMA COMMA COMMA COMMA CHAMELEON

Ah, the comma—the most versatile (and therefore confusing) punctuation mark in the English language. Many people were taught to use a comma when they would naturally pause in a sentence, but that "rule" is wrong. It's a decent way to guess if you have absolutely no idea whether you need a comma, but it's not a rule and won't reliably lead you to the right answer. You'll end up using commas like confetti, throwing them around whenever the mood strikes you. Let me get you started on your path to redemption.

SERIAL COMMA

The **serial comma** (also known as the Oxford comma) comes before the final conjunction in a list. Whether to use the serial comma is often a style decision, which is why so many people are confused.

Although the serial comma isn't always necessary, I favor it because often it does add clarity, and I believe in having a simple, consistent style instead of trying to decide whether you need something on a case-by-case basis. The serial comma makes even simple lists easier to read.

> Aardvark and Squiggly love chocolate, hiking, and fishing. (with serial comma)

> Aardvark and Squiggly love chocolate, hiking and fishing. (without serial comma)

Sure, the second sentence (without the serial comma) isn't confusing in this very basic list of items, but even if you are against—or have a teacher who is against—the serial comma, you have to use one when leaving it out would create confusion. This easily happens when the items in the list have internal conjunctions or are complex in some other way.

Here's a sentence that could mean different things with and without the final comma because one of the list items has an internal conjunction:

> Squiggly was proud of his new muffin recipes: blueberry, peanut butter and chocolate chip and coconut.

Without a serial comma, you wouldn't know whether the last item is a combination of peanut butter and chocolate chip or a combination of chocolate chip and coconut. You can make the meaning clear in two ways: place the final comma after *peanut butter* or after *chocolate chip*, or rewrite the sentence so there is no ambiguity.

> Squiggly was proud of his new muffin recipes: blueberry, peanut butter, and chocolate chip and coconut.
> (The combo is chocolate chip and coconut.)

> Squiggly was proud of his new muffin recipes: blueberry, peanut butter and chocolate chip, and coconut.
> (The combo is peanut butter and chocolate chip.)

Leaving out the comma can also be confusing when the later items in the list can describe an earlier item. A great (and classic) example is the made-up book dedication *To my parents, Ayn Rand and God*.

A reasonable reader would assume there are four entities being thanked: Mom, Dad, Ayn Rand, and God; but without the serial comma, you could also conclude that the two parents are Ayn Rand and God. A serial comma clears up any confusion: *To my parents, Ayn Rand, and God*.

Occasionally, there are situations in which even a serial comma doesn't make the meaning clear. Consider this sentence: *I went to see Zack, an officer and a gentleman*.

Without the serial comma, *I went to see Zack, an officer and a gentleman* could mean that Zack is both an officer and a gentleman, or that I went to see three people: Zack, an unnamed officer, and an unnamed gentleman.

With the serial comma, *I went to see Zack, an officer, and a gentleman* could still mean two different things. It could mean I went to see three people (Zack, an unnamed officer, and an unnamed gentleman), or it could mean I went to see two people (Zack, who is an officer, and an unnamed gentleman). The best solution is to rewrite.

Bottom line? I favor using the serial comma all the time. And sometimes sorting out your meaning is just too much for one little comma and the best option is to rewrite your sentence.

3-7 ADJECTIVES AND COMMAS

Using commas with multiple adjectives is another tricky area; fortunately, the rules are straightforward.

1. Can you put the word *and* between the adjectives and have the sentence still make sense?
2. Can you reverse the order of the adjectives and have the sentence still make sense?

If you can do those two things, then use a comma between the adjectives because each adjective is describing the noun. These are called **coordinate adjectives**.

> Aardvark is a hairy and small mammal.
> Aardvark is a small and hairy mammal.
> Aardvark is a small, hairy mammal.

You can use *and* between the adjectives and reverse the order in the examples above, so you use a comma.

When your adjectives don't meet the above criteria—when you can't reverse the order or put *and* between them and have them still make sense—they are called **cumulative adjectives**. They are adjectives that build on each other, and you don't put a comma between them. For example, in the following sentence you can't change the order of the adjectives *four*, *green*, and *Easter*:

Squiggly found four green Easter eggs.
Squiggly found green four Easter eggs. (yuck!)
Squiggly found Easter green four eggs. (yuck!)
Squiggly found green Easter four eggs. (yuck!)

Remember, you can test whether you're dealing with cumulative or coordinate adjectives by checking if it's possible to switch them around.

The "ly" Adjective Challenge

Sometimes you'll use adjectives that look like adverbs. That's a challenge—is the word that ends in *ly* an adjective and you use a comma, or is it an adverb, meaning you don't need a comma?

In the following sentence, *daily* is an adjective modifying the noun *run*; therefore, it is OK to use a comma:

Aardvark took a long, daily run.

But in this sentence, *daily* is an adverb modifying the verb *trains*; therefore, don't use a comma:

Aardvark trains hard daily.

The sentence doesn't make sense if you reverse the order of *hard* and *daily*.

Aardvark trains daily hard. (yuck)

In the following sentence, *friendly* is an adjective modifying the noun *beast*; therefore, it is OK to use a comma:

Squiggly is a friendly, yellow beast.

In this next example, *fiercely* is an adverb modifying the adjective *loyal*; therefore, don't use a comma:

> Aardvark is a fiercely loyal friend.

Note that you couldn't reverse the order of *fiercely* and *loyal* or put *and* between them.

> Aardvark is a loyal fiercely friend. (yuck)
> Aardvark is a fiercely and loyal friend. (more yuck)

3-8 PUTTING COMMAS TO WORK IN YOUR SENTENCES

When we talked about sentences in Chapter Two, I included conjunctions, phrases, independent clauses, and so on, but I didn't tell you how to use punctuation with all these sentence parts. Now is the time.

Commas and Coordinating Conjunctions

One of the most common places to use commas is where two main clauses (independent clauses) are connected by a coordinating conjunction (the FANBOYS—see section 1-36). You usually need a comma before the conjunction.

Squiggly ran to the forest is a complete sentence by itself. *Aardvark chased the squirrels* is a complete sentence by itself.

If the two events happened at the same time, you can use *and* to connect them. Join two main clauses with a comma and a conjunction.

> Squiggly ran to the forest, and Aardvark chased the squirrels.

Here's another example:

> Squiggly ran to the forest, but Aardvark chased the squirrels.

Again, these two events are connected in time, and the conjunction *but* joins them.

When don't you use a comma with the coordinating conjunctions? When you aren't joining two main clauses (remember, those are things that could be complete sentences if they are alone), you don't need a comma.

> Squiggly ran to the forest, and chased the squirrels.
> (wrong)

Squiggly ran to the forest is a complete sentence, but *chased the squirrels* is not. There's no subject.

In most cases, you need a subject in the second half of the sentence to use the comma. The comma in the sentence above is wrong because there is no main clause after it.

The only time you might use a comma in a sentence like the one above is if the second part of the sentence is in stark contrast to the first part.

> Squiggly cowered under a rock, but felt brave.
> (comma allowed because of contrast)

I don't make the rules; I just explain them.

One question that always comes up is whether to follow the conjunction with a comma when you use it to start a sentence. A comma is not required after the conjunction unless there's an aside that would require commas immediately after the conjunction.

> And I love the holidays. (no comma required after *And*)
> And, despite the extra work, I love the holidays.

(See sidebar box in section 2-6 for more about sentence fragments and section 2-14 for more about starting sentences with conjunctions.)

Never Comma Splice

Do not use a comma between two independent clauses (sentences) without a conjunction. It's an error called a **comma splice**, or a comma fault.

It's easy to see why it is called a comma splice: the comma is used to splice together two complete sentences when that isn't the function of a comma.

> Squiggly ran to the forest, Aardvark chased the squirrels. (I'm shocked! Where is the coordinating conjunction? Comma splice! Epic fail!)

The good news is that it's easy to fix a comma splice once you recognize the problem. There's a whole bag of tricks to choose from—periods, commas and conjunctions, semicolons, dashes, and colons. For example, because the two clauses are complete sentences, you could use a period where you had a comma.

> Squiggly ran to the forest. Aardvark chased the squirrels.

Here are the other options:

> Squiggly ran to the forest, but Aardvark chased the squirrels.

> Squiggly ran to the forest; Aardvark chased the squirrels.
>
> Squiggly ran to the forest: Aardvark chased the squirrels.
>
> Squiggly ran to the forest—Aardvark chased the squirrels.

The last two sentences are not the best examples of how to use colons and dashes (see sections 3-12 and 3-16), but in some cases comma splices can be repaired with those two punctuation marks.

Grammar Girl feels much better now.

Run-on Sentences: Running on Empty

Run-on sentences are, in some ways, the opposite of comma splices. Instead of using the wrong punctuation, they occur when you don't use any punctuation between two sentences. Many people mistakenly believe that run-on sentences are just long sentences. Actually, they are sentences that are smashed together without any punctuation. For that reason they are also sometimes called fused sentences. The following sentence is a run-on because it doesn't have the proper internal punctuation:

> You're about halfway through this book you should be smarter by now.

Think of punctuation as different elements in a toolbox. To fix sentences, you just pick the right tool. For run-on sentences, you can choose from periods, semicolons, dashes, colons, and commas with coordinating conjunctions.

> You're about halfway through this book. You should be smarter by now.
>
> You're about halfway through this book; you should be smarter by now.
>
> You're about halfway through this book, and you should be smarter by now.

You're about halfway through this book—you should be smarter by now.

You're about halfway through this book: you should be smarter by now.

A colon and dash aren't the best choices for the last two sentences, but they can be used to repair some run-on sentences.

Commas and Subordinating Conjunctions

Not all conjunctions deserve a comma. Subordinating conjunctions join subordinate (or dependent) clauses to the main clause. (See sections 1-38 and 2-4 for more on subordinating conjunctions.) You don't need a comma between the two clauses when the dependent clause comes after the main clause.

Squiggly ran to the forest because he was scared.

Squiggly ran to the forest is the main clause (a complete sentence), and *because he was scared* is the dependent clause.

We had to get up at four in the morning <u>because</u> Aardvark wanted to go fishing.

I'm going to buckle down at work <u>when</u> we get home from vacation.

An exception to this rule is when the two parts of the sentence are in stark contrast. (Commas are often used to mark contrast when they would otherwise be left out.)

Squiggly was wide awake, <u>despite</u> getting up at four in the morning. (The comma is included because of contrast.)

On the other hand, watch what happens when a subordinating

conjunction starts a sentence. A comma is necessary when the subordinate clause (or dependent clause) comes *before* the main clause.

> When he was scared, Squiggly ran to the forest.
> Although he was scared, Squiggly ran to the forest.

QUICK AND DIRTY TIP

When the dependent clause comes before the main clause, use a comma.

Because he was scared, Squiggly ran to the forest.

When the dependent clause comes after the main clause, don't use a comma.

Squiggly ran to the forest because he was scared.

Commas and Conditional Sentences

Conditional sentences have an *if* clause, such as *If you have any questions, let me know*. The action depends on something else.

If you have any questions, let me know means that you will let me know only if you have questions. If you don't have questions, you won't bother to tell me that you don't.

Like dependent clauses, the rule for conditional sentences is when the "if clause" is at the beginning of the sentence, you need a comma. When the "if clause" is at the end of the sentence, you don't need a comma.

> If you have any questions, let me know.
> Let me know if you have any questions.

Note that you can sometimes substitute *when* for *if*.

If It's Essential, Don't Invite the Comma

Commas are also used to separate parenthetical elements, asides, nonessential elements, appositives, and additional information from the rest of the sentence. In other words, commas offset something that could be left out and not change the meaning of the rest of the sentence.

In some sentences, it's easier to see that you can remove the information and not change the meaning.

> Elizabeth I, the queen of England, was King Henry's daughter.

The queen of England describes Elizabeth, but we already know this, so it could be removed. The main information here is that Elizabeth is Henry's daughter.

> Aardvark's best friend, Squiggly, went to the store.

We know that Aardvark's best friend is Squiggly, so we don't lose any information or meaning if we leave out Squiggly's name.

This sentence, however, is different:

> Aardvark's friend Squiggly went to the store.

The name *Squiggly* identifies specifically **which** of Aardvark's friends went to the store (he has many friends, so it is important to identify the specific one). *Squiggly*, in this sentence, is an essential appositive. (See section 2-19 for more on appositives.)

But what about these two sentences that contain appositives? Remember, appositives can be essential information or extra information.

> My sister Alice loves ice cream.
> My sister, Alice, loves ice cream.

The commas (or lack of them) give you loads of information. In the first sentence, the lack of commas tells you that the speaker has more than one sister, and in this specific sentence, the speaker is telling you about his or her sister Alice. The other sisters may not love ice cream, but you now know that this specific sister—Alice—does.

In the second sentence, the commas tell you that the speaker has only one sister, whose name is Alice. You don't really need to know her name—it's nonessential information. The important information in this sentence is that the speaker's one sister loves ice cream.

What if the sentence was rewritten?

Alice, my sister, loves ice cream.

Sister is the extra information, clarifying who Alice is. For the writer, it's more important for you to know that Alice loves ice cream.

Appositives can be tricky, and commas are always tricky, so when faced with an appositive, you need to ask yourself, "Essential or extra?" If the appositive is extra information and can be deleted without changing the meaning of the sentence, then use commas. If it's essential, then don't use commas.

QUICK AND DIRTY TIP

The rule for appositives is if the information is essential, you don't use commas. If it is extra, you use commas. Remember: extra information, extra commas.

Defragmenting the Fragment: The Comma as a Superhero

Sometimes a single comma has the power to turn a fragment into a sentence.

After the dog barked. (a dependent clause, otherwise known as a fragment)

After, the dog barked. (*After* is an introductory phrase, and **the dog barked** is a sentence.)

This won't work with every subordinating conjunction, however. Adding a comma to this sentence still leaves you with a fragment:

Because, the dog barked. (wrong)

Commas with Interjections

Interjections at the beginnings of sentences are followed by commas (or exclamation points if you want to be more dramatic, or periods if you want to be more final).

Oh, he's coming along too?
Yes! I do want to go to the beach.
No. I don't want to go now.

Commas and Direct Address: You Talkin' to Me?

In dialogue, use commas when directly addressing someone by name. Depending on how you write the sentence, the comma will be before or after the name.

Put down your pencil this minute, John.
John, put down your pencil this minute.
Hi, John. How are you?

If you use a person's title as the name, use the comma when addressing the person directly.

Captain, I'm only a country doctor.

Commas and Dates

When writing out the date, separate the day of the month from the year with a comma. Also use a comma after the year.

> Squiggly thinks he met Aardvark on July 14, 2008,
> at a rock concert.

If you leave out any part of the date, leave out the commas.

> Squiggly thinks he met Aardvark around July 14
> at a rock concert, but he can't remember the exact
> year.

> Squiggly thinks he met Aardvark in July 2008
> at a rock concert.

Commas and Numbers

Insert a comma when numbers are over 999, such as 1,203. This rule does not apply to dates.

Commas and Locations

Commas are necessary when writing about a city and a state. The comma goes after the city and after the state.

> Squiggly flew to St. Louis, Missouri, to visit the
> Bowling Hall of Fame.

E.G. and I.E.

If you use the abbreviations *i.e.* and *e.g.*, use a comma afterward; *i.e.* and *e.g.* are both abbreviations for Latin terms.

E.g. means "for example," so you use it to introduce an example.

> Aardvark likes card games, e.g., bridge and crazy eights.

> Squiggly visited Ivy League colleges, e.g., Harvard
> and Yale.

Those sentences tell you that bridge and crazy eights are just a couple of the games Aardvark likes and that Harvard and Yale are just a couple of the colleges Squiggly visited.

On the other hand, *i.e.* means "that is" or "in other words," so you use it to introduce a further clarification.

> Squiggly had no plans (i.e., he was free).

The reason for the comma after *i.e.* and *e.g.* is that you'd place a comma after the words *for example* and *that is*, so you should use it after the abbreviations for those words.

Commas and Quotations

You usually use commas to introduce dialogue with tags such as *he said* and *she asked*.

> Aardvark asked, "Who stole the chocolate?"

Don't use a comma when the quotation flows as part of the sentence—for example, when you introduce a quotation with words such as *that* or *begins with* or *starts*—thereby making the quotation part of your sentence.

> Aardvark knew that the *Peeve Avenger Manual* begins with "Peeves are even more stupid than they look."

Here's an example of a partial quotation that is part of the sentence and therefore doesn't need a comma (although partial quotations like this are often discouraged, and you should generally rewrite the sentence in one of the two formats above):

> Squiggly said Aardvark was "not the cheeriest denizen of the forest."

FYI:
COMMA SUMMARY

Some of the ways to use the comma are as follows:

- in a list
  The American flag is red, white, and blue.

- between coordinate adjectives that can be flipped and can be joined by *and*
  Aardvark is a small, blue mammal.

- between two main clauses joined by a coordinating conjunction
  Squiggly ran to the forest, and Aardvark chased the squirrels.

- in sentences that start with subordinating conjunctions
  Although he was scared, Squiggly ran to the forest.

- to emphasize contrast
  Squiggly was wide awake, *despite* getting up at four in the morning.

- with conditional sentences starting with "if clauses"
  If you have any questions, let me know.

- with nonessential appositives
  Aardvark's best friend, Squiggly, went to the store.

- with nonessential clauses and phrases
  Diamonds, which are expensive, are often used in wedding rings.

- after interjections
  Oh, he's coming along too?

- in a direct address
  John, put down your pencil this minute.

- with dates
  Squiggly met Aardvark July 14, 2008, at a rock concert.

- in numbers over 999
  1,203

- with cities and states
  Squiggly flew to St. Louis, Missouri, to visit the Bowling Hall of Fame.

- after *e.g.* or *i.e.*
  Aardvark likes card games, e.g., bridge and crazy eights.

- to introduce dialogue
  Squiggly said, "Aardvark didn't steal the chocolate. I did."

POP QUIZ

Which is the correct sentence?

1. Grammar Girl knowing she was spreading good grammar throughout the universe, couldn't help but be happy.
2. Grammar Girl, knowing she was spreading good grammar, throughout the universe, couldn't help but be happy.
3. Grammar Girl, knowing she was spreading good grammar throughout the universe couldn't help but be happy.
4. Grammar Girl, knowing she was spreading good grammar throughout the universe, couldn't help but be happy.

Answer: 4

SEMICOLONS: THE TRUE SENTENCE SPLICERS

Semicolons separate things or bring them together, depending on how you see the world.

If you have two separate sentences that are closely related to each other, you can use the semicolon to unite them in one big, happy sentence.

Or you can see semicolons as separating two main clauses that are closely related to each other but can stand on their own as sentences if you wanted them to.

> It was below zero; Squiggly wondered if he would freeze to death.

> It was below zero. Squiggly wondered if he would freeze to death.

I think of semicolons as sentence splicers: they splice sentences together. Although *splice* sounds as though it means to separate or cut apart, it actually means "to unite."

One reason you may choose to use a semicolon instead of a period is that you want to add variety to your sentence structure. For example, if you thought you had too many short, choppy sentences in a row, you could add variety by using a semicolon to string together two main clauses into one longer sentence.

When you use a semicolon, the main clauses should be closely related. You wouldn't write *It was below zero; Squiggly had pizza for dinner*, because those two main clauses have nothing to do with each other. In fact, the other reason to use a semicolon instead of a period is to draw attention to the relationship between the two clauses.

SEMICOLONS WITH COORDINATING CONJUNCTIONS 3-10

An important thing to remember is that (with two exceptions) you never use semicolons with coordinating conjunctions such as *and*, *or*, and *but*. If you're joining two main clauses with a coordinating conjunction, use a comma.

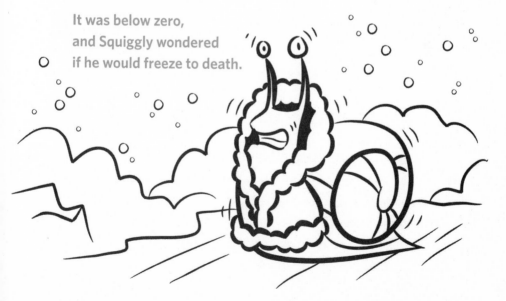

It was below zero,
and Squiggly wondered
if he would freeze to death.

The first exception is when you are writing a list and need commas in some or all of the items within the list.

> The winners are Herbie in Des Moines, Iowa; Matt in Irvine, California; and Jan in Seattle, Washington.

Because each item requires a comma to separate the city from the state, you have to use a semicolon to separate the items themselves. Here's another example:

> Herbie likes oysters more than clams, hot dogs more than hamburgers, and mustard more than ketchup; Matt likes fries more than potato chips, root beer more than cola, and cookies more than ice cream; and Jan likes cake more than cupcakes, pizza more than spaghetti, and milk shakes more than soda.

Because of the serial comma within each clause and because the sentence contains three main clauses, the semicolons make the sentence less confusing, although it's admittedly quite awkward.

The second exception is that it's OK to use semicolons with coordinating conjunctions when you're combining long clauses with internal commas.

> Wading through the river, Grammar Girl wondered whether Sir Fragalot, the knight who couldn't speak in complete sentences, would enjoy fishing; but when she tripped over a rock, nearly knocking herself out, she forgot about Sir Fragalot.

SEMICOLONS WITH CONJUNCTIVE ADVERBS

3-11

Finally, use a semicolon when you have a **conjunctive adverb** joining two main clauses. Conjunctive adverbs are words such as *however*, *therefore*, and *indeed*, and they typically show some kind of relationship between the two main clauses. For a list of common conjunctive adverbs, see Appendix section A-2.

Aardvark is on vacation; therefore, Squiggly has to do extra work in this chapter.

Squiggly doesn't mind doing the extra work; however, he would like to be thanked.

POP QUIZ

Choose the correct sentence.

1. Ralph crossed the finish line first, and won the race.
2. Ralph crossed the finish line first; and he won the race.
3. Ralph crossed the finish line first; Squiggly lost the race.
4. Ralph crossed the finish line first, Squiggly lost the race.

Answer: 3

THE COLON: I CAN'T WAIT TO READ WHAT COMES NEXT

3-12

Anticipation—that's the colon. The colon signals that what comes next is directly related to the previous sentence.

COLONS IN SENTENCES

3-13

When you use colons in sentences, the most important thing to remember is that colons must go after statements that are main clauses. Never use a colon after a sentence fragment.

Squiggly has two favorite pets: Fluffy and Rascal.

Squiggly has two favorite pets is a complete sentence all by itself.

The items after the colon expand on or clarify what came before it. I referred to Squiggly's favorite pets before the colon and then specifically named them afterward.

You can also use a colon between two main clauses when the second one expands on or clarifies the first one.

The band was wildly popular: they sold out the Coliseum.

QUICK AND DIRTY TIP

When deciding whether a colon is acceptable, test whether you can replace it with the word *namely*.

Squiggly has two favorite pets, *namely*, Fluffy and Rascal.

Most of the time, if you can replace a colon with the word *namely*, then the colon is the right choice.

It would be wrong to write

Squiggly's favorite pets are: Fluffy and Rascal.

Squiggly's favorite pets are is not a complete sentence by itself. You can fix that problem by taking away the colon or adding the words **the following** or **as follows** after your sentence fragment.

For example, it would be fine to write

Squiggly's favorite pets are Fluffy and Rascal. (no colon)

Squiggly's favorite pets are as follows: Fluffy and Rascal. (adding *as follows*)

Squiggly's favorite pets are as follows is a complete sentence.

Dos and Don'ts of Colon Use in Sentences

<u>Do</u> use a colon before a list if the clause before the colon is a complete sentence.

> I want to talk to famous dead people: Abraham Lincoln, Eleanor Roosevelt, and Martin Luther King Jr.

<u>Don't</u> use a colon right after a verb.

> The people I want to talk to are: Abraham Lincoln, Eleanor Roosevelt, and Martin Luther King Jr. (wrong)

> The people I want to talk to are Abraham Lincoln, Eleanor Roosevelt, and Martin Luther King Jr. (right)

<u>Don't</u> use a colon after a preposition and before a list.

> I want to talk to: Abraham Lincoln, Eleanor Roosevelt, and Martin Luther King Jr. (wrong)

> I want to talk to Abraham Lincoln, Eleanor Roosevelt, and Martin Luther King Jr. (right)

COLONS IN LISTS

3-14

Don't let lists confuse you when it comes to colons. The rules are the same whether you're writing lists or a sentence. Use a colon when the clause could be a complete sentence on its own or when you could use the word *namely* before the list.

> Squiggly has two favorite pets:
> * Fluffy
> * Rascal

(correct because the colon follows a complete sentence)

> Squiggly's two favorite pets are
> * Fluffy
> * Rascal

(correct because there is no colon after the verb *are*)

Colons and Capitalization

Should you capitalize the first word after a colon?

The answer is that it's a style issue, and it depends on what is following the colon.

Although the most conservative grammarians would say that you should capitalize the first word after a colon when the colon introduces a complete sentence, other grammarians say capitalization isn't necessary.

Because you never capitalize the first word after a colon if it is introducing something that isn't a complete sentence, I find it easier to adopt the less conservative lowercase rule for introducing complete sentences.

All I have to remember is that the first word after a colon is always in lowercase (unless, of course, it is a proper name or something else that's always capitalized).

But remember this is a style choice, so your teacher or employer may prefer a different style.

3-15

COLONS IN A VARIETY OF SITUATIONS

Salutations

Colons are also used after salutations in business letters.

Dear Mr. Smith:

Time

Colons are used in time to separate hours from minutes (when you don't spell out the numbers).

I left the house at 4:59.

Titles of Books

Colons are used in book titles, especially to separate the main title from the subtitle.

> Aardvark just finished writing *Grammar: An Anteater's Guide to All You Need to Know.*

Dialogue in Plays

Colons are used in scripts for dramatic presentations.

> AARDVARK: Get out of my house!
> SQUIGGLY: But I have nowhere to go.

Ratios

In math or at the racetrack, colons are very handy when writing out ratios.

> The horse had a 5:1 chance of winning.

Colon? Semicolon? Colon? Semicolon? Which to Choose?

What is the difference between a semicolon and a colon?

1. A colon introduces or defines something, and a semicolon shows that two clauses are related. Here's an example of a sentence that needs a colon:

> Squiggly was fixated on something: chocolate.

Here's a clear example of a sentence that needs a semicolon:

> Squiggly was fixated; he couldn't get his mind off chocolate.

The first sentence needs a colon because the second part (chocolate) defines the first part (the thing Squiggly can't get out of his head). The second sentence needs a semicolon because the two parts are strongly related. The second clause explains what is going on in the first clause.

2. A semicolon joins things of equal weight. A colon joins things of equal or unequal weight.

For example, you can use either a semicolon or a colon to join two main clauses, but you can only use a colon to join a main clause with a lone noun.

You wouldn't use a semicolon in this sentence because the two parts are unequal:

Squiggly missed only one friend: Aardvark.

You would use a semicolon in this sentence because the two parts are equal:

Squiggly missed only one friend; he missed Aardvark.

POP QUIZ

Which of the following are correct sentences?

1. Ralph crossed the finish line first; and won the race.
2. Ralph crossed the finish line first; he won the race.
3. Ralph crossed the finish line first, and Squiggly lost the race.
4. Ralph crossed the finish line first. Squiggly lost the race.

Answers: 2, 3, 4

DASHES: I'M DASHING OFF TO BUY A GRAMMAR BOOK

The difference between a colon and a dash is subtle. They can both serve to introduce a related element after a sentence, but a dash is a more sensational and informal mark than a colon.

Think of a colon as part of the sentence that just ambles along. It informs readers that something more is coming along shortly.

> Squiggly has two favorite pets (and now I'm going to tell you who they are): Fluffy and Rascal.

A dash, on the other hand—well, it's quite dramatic. A dashing young man is certainly not an ordinary young man, and if you're dashing off to the store, you're not just going to the store, you're going in a flurry. A dash interrupts the flow of the sentence and tells the reader to get ready for an important or dramatic statement.

If you added a dash to the "pets" sentence, it would conceptually read something like this:

> Squiggly has two favorite pets (wait for it; wait for it)—Fluffy and Rascal. Wow!

Given that there isn't anything exciting about Squiggly's pets, a dash may not be the best choice here, but it wouldn't be wrong. It would be a better choice if that sentence were part of a mystery novel in which only some of Squiggly's pets were missing, and they were Fluffy and Rascal. Then it could be a dramatic announcement that those were his favorite pets, and a dash would make more sense.

Dashes can also be used like commas or parentheses to set off part of a sentence that is an aside. When you use dashes to set off a parenthetical element, you're using the strongest method possible to draw attention to it, so be sure it merits the drama.

> Frank—Ed's evil twin brother—now had the upper hand.

You can use dashes when you write long appositives that have many commas.

> My brother—the tall one with red hair, clown shoes, baseball mitt, plaid shirt, and striped pants— really likes you.

When you write dialogue, dashes can be used to show an interruption of thought or change of direction. These tend to be stronger breaks than those indicated by ellipses.

> "Um . . . my brother really likes you. He said you should— Look! An ice cream truck!"

(You can use ellipses for this too. See section 3-20.)

Don't overuse the dash. If you do, it will be like crying wolf. Readers may stop believing that everything you say is so vitally important.

(See Appendix section A-6 for information about another kind of dash.)

3-17 THE HYPHEN: A LOOK-IT-UP PUNCTUATION MARK

You use a hyphen to split a word (between syllables) at the end of a line, but you also use a hyphen to join some compound words.

A **compound word** is a word made up of two words—*eyelash* (*eye lash*), *billboard* (*bill board*), *airplane* (*air plane*).

The rules about when to hyphenate a compound word are a bit squidgy. Well, actually, they're a lot squidgy. The problem is that compound words go through an evolution from open compound (two separate words) to hyphenated compound to closed compound (one word with the two parts shoved together)—and sometimes back again—and the changes can seem arbitrary.

For example, when the *Shorter Oxford English Dictionary* was released in 2007, it eliminated 16,000 hyphenated words. Some words (*leap-frog*) advanced to closed-compound form (*leapfrog*), and other words (*pot-belly*) reverted to open-compound form (*pot belly*).

The best advice I can give you is to pick a dictionary and consult it when you aren't sure whether to hyphenate a compound word.

You often use a hyphen between **compound adjectives** that come directly *before* the noun they modify. Compound adjectives are two or more words that together create an adjective. A compound adjective should be understood as one word. But do not hyphenate these adjectives when they come *after* the noun they modify.

> They are in a <u>long-term</u> relationship.
> Their relationship is <u>long term</u>.

When two adjectives modify a noun, sometimes the sentence could be read two ways or be initially confusing to a reader, so you can use a hyphen to clarify which words go together:

> Grammar Girl shopped at the silver-jewelry cart.

That sentence makes it clear that I like silver jewelry.

Take away the hyphen and the sentence could have a completely different meaning.

> Grammar Girl shopped at the silver jewelry cart.

Now you can't tell whether the jewelry or the cart is silver.

Confusion also reigns when you have three adjectives in a row and two of them are connected. If you don't hyphenate the compound adjective, the meaning isn't clear.

She coveted the green stitched denim jacket. (Huh?)

If I read the sentence above, I'd be confused. Is it the stitching or the jacket that is green?

She coveted the green-stitched denim jacket.
(OK, the stitching is green.)

She coveted the green stitched-denim jacket.
(OK, the jacket is green.)

Hyphens Through the Ages

If you need to write out ages, notice how hyphens are used. When the age is an adjective that comes before the noun and modifies the noun, or when the age is a noun, hyphenate.

Five-year-old Squiggly eats ice cream.
The yellow five-year-old loves ice cream.
Squiggly is a five-year-old.

(You use a hyphen in the third example because *snail* is implied—a five-year-old snail—so the hyphenated adjective is coming before the implied noun it modifies.)

When the age is part of an adjective phrase after the noun, don't hyphenate.

Squiggly is five years old.

ADVERBS AND HYPHENS DO NOT MIX

Hyphenate adjectives that work together when they appear before the noun, but don't hyphenate adverbs.

He is a <u>clear-thinking</u> person.

He is a person who thinks clearly; *clear-thinking* is an adjective.

He likes only <u>individually wrapped</u> cheese.

Here, *individually* is an adverb describing how the cheese is wrapped, so you don't use a hyphen.

POP QUIZ

Choose the correct sentence.

1. The horribly-sunburned aardvark carefully rubbed the coconut-smelling lotion on his lobster-red arms.
2. The horribly sunburned aardvark carefully rubbed the coconut-smelling lotion on his lobster-red arms.
3. The horribly, sunburned aardvark carefully rubbed the coconut-smelling lotion on his lobster, red arms.
4. The horribly sunburned aardvark carefully rubbed the coconut, smelling lotion on his lobster red arms.

Answer: 2

HYPHENS WITH VERBS AND OTHER CONSTRUCTIONS

A hyphen may eliminate confusion when it is used to clarify pronunciation. See how these two verbs mean different things with and without the hyphen:

I need to re-press my jeans.
(meaning I need to iron them again)

I need to repress those memories.
(meaning I need to suppress those memories)

Despite the vast wiggle room in hyphen land, there are a few solid rules. You can confidently use a hyphen when you are

joining a prefix to a word that must be capitalized
- anti-American
- un-American
- pre-Mesozoic

joining a letter or numeral to a word
- X-ray
- A-list
- T-shirt
- 100-foot

joining a prefix to a date
- pre-1400
- mid-1960s

separating words with the same three letters in a row
- fall-like (not falllike)
- shell-like (not shelllike)

writing out numbers from twenty-one to ninety-nine
- thirty-five
- sixty-four
- ninety-three

Some prefixes—such as *ex*, *near*, *mid*, *self*, and *all*—usually demand a hyphen. (If you've never met a demanding prefix, consider yourself lucky.)

> My great-grandmother's ex-husband—he was born in the mid-1800s—was self-employed and all-knowing.

Some words are meant to be read as a single unit, so a hyphen is helpful.

> The California-Nevada border runs through Lake Tahoe.

Use a hyphen when writing fractions as adjectives or adverbs, not as nouns.

> His one-third share of the treasure belonged to her. (adjective)

> He gave her one third of the treasure. (noun)

Suspended Hyphens

All right, are you ready for this? You can suspend hyphens. (No, I don't mean you can hang them by their toes, although hyphens are so complicated sometimes I want to!) **Suspended** or **suspensive hyphens** are used with adjectives. Let's say you have a simple sentence.

> Squiggly ordered the blue-striped scarf for Aardvark.

But then Squiggly decides to order striped scarves in many different colors for all his friends.

To write this in the easiest way possible, you'd use one word, but it is connected to a list of words that describe one noun.

> Squiggly ordered the blue-, red-, yellow-, and pink-striped scarves for his friends.

This means that Squiggly ordered the blue-striped, red-striped, yellow-striped, and pink-striped scarves for his friends. Four different scarves, each striped with a different color, but it's a lot easier to read it when you use suspended hyphens

Suspended hyphens are economical—there's no need to name the second part of the compound when you're going to get to it in a second. These hyphens say be patient; it will show up soon.

> Do you want a one- or two-bedroom apartment?

> Please pick up a ten- or twelve-foot pipe at the hardware store.

It's fine to occasionally make up an adjective using a long string of hyphenated words for effect, but don't overdo it to the point that you become an irritating hyphenate-everything-in-sight-for-no-reason writer. You can also achieve the same effect by enclosing the words in quotation marks without hyphens.

And, I must repeat, when you are unsure or the tiniest bit doubtful, or even if you have no doubt, check the dictionary to see how to spell compound words, words with prefixes, and words with suffixes.

Beware! A Hyphen Does Not a Dash Make

Do not confuse the hyphen with the dash. A hyphen is not a junior dash. Using them interchangeably creates chaos in the world of grammar. They have very different jobs.

POP QUIZ

Choose the correct sentence.

1. Because his exceptionally sloppy room bothered his neat-freak mother, he hung a warning sign on his door to avoid their usual clean your room fights.
2. Because his exceptionally sloppy room bothered his neat-freak mother, he hung a warning sign on his door to avoid their usual clean-your-room fights.
3. Because his exceptionally sloppy room bothered his neat freak mother, he hung a warning sign on his door to avoid their usual clean-your-room fights.
4. Because his exceptionally-sloppy room bothered his neat-freak mother, he hung a warning sign on his door to avoid their usual clean your room fights.

Answer: 2

ELLIPSES

3-20

You've seen those three dots that follow a sentence or clause or are plunked down in the middle of a sentence, right? Those dots are called **ellipsis points**, and three dots together are called an *ellipsis* or an *ellipsis mark.* The omission itself is also called an *ellipsis*, and multiple omissions are called *ellipses.*

The most common and formal use of this punctuation is to indicate an omission. If you're quoting someone and you want to shorten the quotation, you use ellipsis points to show where you've dropped words or sentences.

Here's a quotation from the book *Our Mutual Friend* by Charles Dickens: "I cannot help it; reason has nothing to do with it; I love her against reason."

Now, far be it from me to edit Dickens, but if my English paper can be only three pages, I'd be tempted to shorten it to this: "I cannot help it . . . I love her against reason."

That middle part—*reason has nothing to do with it*—seems redundant, and taking it out doesn't change the meaning. Dot-dot-dot, and it's gone, which saves me seven words. Clearly, literature and term papers are not the same thing.

Integrity is essential when using ellipsis points in this way. It's fine to tighten a long quotation by omitting unnecessary words, but it's important that you don't change the meaning. It's wrong to omit words to misrepresent what someone said. For example, imagine what an unethical writer could do with the following quotation:

> "Squiggly's acting would make your heart sing—if you were lucky enough not to be in the theater."

It would be easy to make the sentence sound as if the writer loved Squiggly's acting. Here's the revised quotation:

> "Squiggly's acting would make your heart sing . . ."

See? Chop off the qualifier at the end, and you've got a completely different quotation. Or remove only one word:

> "Squiggly's acting would make your heart sing—if you were lucky enough . . . to be in the theater."

Of course, these are obvious and dreadful examples; you would never do that! But be careful not to introduce more subtle changes in meaning when you use ellipsis points (and when you are editing quotations in general).

Ellipses are also used like dashes to show hesitating speech in dialogue. (See section 3-16.)

> "Um . . . you know my brother? Well . . . he really, really . . . uh . . . likes you."

Finally, ellipsis marks can show that something is being left unsaid or that the speaker's or writer's thoughts trailed off. Note that when this happens at the end of a sentence, no period is required after the ellipsis.

> Squiggly said he'd call, but . . .

FORMATTING ELLIPSES

3-21

Now that you know how to use ellipses, you need to know how to make them. An ellipsis consists of exactly three dots called ellipsis points—never two dots, never four dots—just three dots.

Most style guides call for a space between the dots. Type period-space-period-space-period. Just make sure your ellipsis doesn't get broken up and spread out over two lines. If you want to get fancy, most fonts have an ellipsis that you can insert as a special character.

Also, there should always be a space on each side of an ellipsis.

If, for example, you're writing dialogue and you're omitting something that comes after a complete sentence, put the period at the end of the sentence just as you normally would, then type a space, and then insert your ellipsis points.

> We've lost the game. . . . We always lose.

You treat it the same way—put a space on each side—if the ellipsis comes before other kinds of sentence-ending punctuation marks such as a question mark.

> Is Aardvark coming home on Thursday?
> Is Aardvark coming home . . . ?

Fortunately, most style guides don't call for an ellipsis when you omit something at the end of a quotation, so you don't have to deal with it too often. Putting an ellipsis at the beginning of a quotation is also usually not necessary, but again it is a matter of style.

ASTERISKS: SEEING STARS

The asterisk is that little star above the 8 key on your keyboard, and the word *asterisk* actually comes from the Latin and Greek words for "little star." It's pronounced "aster-isk." It's common to hear people call it an "aster-ick" or "aster-ix," but the correct pronunciation is "aster-isk."

ASTEREXASPERATION: FOLLOWING THROUGH

You place an **asterisk** after something you want to comment on or qualify. My first rule for using an asterisk is to make sure it refers to something at the bottom of the page. It makes me crazy when ads have an asterisk next to some offer, and then you can't find what it means. More than once I've seen something such as *Jeans, 20% off,* and then nothing else on the page to indicate what the asterisk means. Are jeans only on sale Wednesday? Only if you buy two pairs? You have no idea; it's sketchy.

When you combine an asterisk with other punctuation marks, the asterisk goes after every punctuation mark except the dash.

> Squiggly won the pie-eating contest by two pies.*

> Out-eating last year's champion by two pies,*
> Squiggly won the contest.

> Squiggly out-ate last year's champion by two pies*—he was on his way to the record books.

> *The winning pies were blueberry and gooseberry.

QUOTATION MARKS: YOU CAN QUOTE ME

The most common use of **double quotation marks** is to surround direct quotations or spoken words. Something inside quotation marks is assumed to be *exactly* what the person being quoted said or wrote.

"I hope the movie starts soon," said Squiggly.

> I hope the movie starts soon.

Indirect quotations are not word-for-word and don't need the quotation marks.

Aardvark said that he hoped the movie would start soon.

Let's say that the following is the original or direct quotation:

In his school newspaper, Smith wrote, "The Vykings beat us by 50, and I mean pointaroos not percent, last week at our glorious, magnificent, and bombastic home stadium."

If you make changes, you must indicate them with ellipses (also see section 3-20) and brackets (see section 3-31). If the quotation has an error, you can use the abbreviation *sic* (which is Latin for "thus; so") in square brackets, which indicates the error was made by the speaker or original writer and not by the current writer.

> In his school newspaper, Smith wrote, "The Vykings [*sic*] beat us by 50 [points] last week at our . . . home stadium." (edited quotation)

> In his school newspaper, Smith noted that the Vikings won by 50 points at the Warriors' beloved home stadium. (paraphrased, indirect quotation)

Typically, if you must make too many changes to a quotation, it is better to paraphrase the statement.

Quotation Versus *Quote*

Quotation is a noun; *quote* is a verb.

It's common to hear people use the verb *quote* as a shortened form of *quotation*, as in *I filled my notebook with quotes from the lecture*, but such use is, in the strictest sense, wrong. It should be *I filled my notebook with quotations from the lecture*.

I agree the correct way sounds kind of pretentious. You aren't going to sound illiterate if you use *quote* incorrectly (and some dictionaries even say *quote* is fine as a noun), but it is still good to know the difference and stick to *quotation* in formal writing. It's a pet peeve for some people.

3-25

QUOTATION MARKS WITH OTHER PUNCTUATION: MIXED COMPANY

Rarely do quotation marks stand alone. They usually involve some other punctuation mark. And, yes, different punctuation marks go inside or outside the quotation marks.

Quotation Marks with Commas and Periods

I'm willing to bet that half of you don't know whether to put periods and commas inside or outside the quotation marks. It's confusing because it's done differently in Britain and America. So, if you're spending time online reading websites written by people in both places, you'll regularly see it done differently. Here's my U.S.-centric memory trick:

> *Inside* the U.S., periods and commas go *inside* the quotation marks. ("Jump in the pond.")

Quotation Marks with Question Marks and Exclamation Points

Where do you put the question mark or exclamation point when you're using quotation marks? It depends on the sentence. Is the whole thing a big question or exclamation, or is only the part in quotation marks a question or exclamation?

If the whole sentence is a question, then you put the question mark outside the quotation mark.

> What do you think Squiggly meant when he said, "The fish swam darkly up the river"?

The whole sentence is a question, so the question mark goes at the very end (outside the quotation mark).

On the other hand, if only the quotation is a question, then the question mark goes inside the quotation mark.

> Squiggly ran up to Aardvark and asked, "Where are the fish?"

The question mark goes inside the quotation mark because the only part of the sentence that is a question is **Where are the fish?** (You don't need a period after the quotation mark. Despite being inside the quotation mark, the question mark serves as the terminal punctuation.) It works the same way with exclamation points.

It helps to remember that the question mark (or exclamation point) stays attached to the question (or exclamation)—whether it makes up the whole sentence or just the quotation.

Quotation Marks with Semicolons and Colons

You probably won't often need to use colons and semicolons with quotation marks, but I, like the Girl Scouts (or is it the Boy Scouts?), believe in being prepared. Colons and semicolons always go outside the quotation marks, no matter how much they beg to be let in.

> Charlie said his room was "off-limits"; nevertheless, I snuck in the moment he left.

> The message on his T-shirt was "I step on snails": the motto of the antisnail movement.

3-26   CAPITALIZATION, COMMAS, AND PERIODS IN CONVERSATION: HOW TO SET UP DIALOGUE

It may look tricky, but it's pretty easy to figure out when to use commas or periods in dialogue. Capitalizing the first word after a quotation mark depends on whether you're in the middle of a spoken sentence or not.

The comma is used before the quotation and after.

> Squiggly said, "Let's go."
> "Let's go," said Squiggly.

But what if Squiggly said more than *Let's go*?

> "Let's go," said Squiggly. "We don't want to be late."

The period follows *Squiggly* because *"Let's go," said Squiggly* is a complete sentence. *We don't want to be late* is a new sentence, so you capitalize *We*.

"Ashley," he said, "you look tired."

The comma is used after *he said* because the spoken sentence wasn't finished yet. The *you* isn't capitalized because the speaker was in the middle of his spoken sentence.

On and On and Back and Forth

Let's say you're writing the great American novel. You will probably have more than one character, and you will include some back and forth between them. It would look like this:

> "No," said Squiggly. "I don't want to go."
> "I don't care what you think. I want you to come," Aardvark insisted.
> Squiggly pulled his arm out of Aardvark's hand.
> "No! No! No!" Squiggly paused before continuing.
> "You never listen to me!"

I didn't say that *I* was able to write the great American novel, but at least my punctuation is correct. I started a new paragraph with each new speaker. The commas and periods are all in their proper places.

If you are quoting a speaker and the comments run a couple of paragraphs, you don't use the ending quotation marks until you are finished quoting that person. However, each new paragraph will have the open quotation marks.

"I didn't say that *I* was able to write the great American novel. But at least my punctuation is correct. I started a new paragraph with each new speaker. The commas and periods are all in their proper places. I had action, dialogue, action, and dialogue. I made good use of punctuation in that paragraph.

"If you are quoting something for a term paper and it runs a couple of paragraphs, you don't use the ending quotation marks

until you are finished quoting that specific section. However, each new paragraph will have the open quotation marks."

DEFINITIONS: YOU CAN QUOTE ME ON THIS

You can use quotation marks for definitions.

> **According to *Merriam-Webster Online*, a dictionary is "a reference source in print or electronic form containing words usually alphabetically arranged along with information about their forms, pronunciations, functions, etymologies, meanings, and syntactical and idiomatic uses."**

Quotation marks are also useful for quoting signs or labels.

> The label read "do not wash," but he did.
> I always think the "yield" sign reads "wield."

marks used as something called "scare quotes," which are quotation marks put around a word to show that the writer doesn't buy into the meaning.

For example, I could write the sentence *Women achieved "equality" when they were granted the right to vote in 1920*.

The quotation marks indicate that although women getting the right to vote was heralded as equality at the time, I don't think it was enough of a gain to merit the word *equality*.

More often, though, scare quotes (which are also sometimes called sneer quotes) are used to impart a sense of irony or disdain. They're especially common when people are being nasty or snarky.

She's so "stylish" with her unwashed hair, last year's clothes, and mismatched socks.

Don't you just hate the "caring" person who said that?

SINGLE QUOTATION MARKS: THE SINGLE LIFE

Single quotation marks are like backup double quotation marks: you pull them out of your bag of tricks when you've already used double quotation marks. The most common use is when you are quoting someone who is quoting someone else. You enclose the primary speaker's comments in double quotation marks, and then you enclose what they are quoting in single quotation marks.

Squiggly said, "Aardvark yelled, 'Watch out,' as the arrow was coming toward me."

If you're ever in the rare position of having to nest another quotation inside a sentence like that, you would use double quotation marks again for the statement inside the single quotation marks.

Squiggly said, "Aardvark yelled, *'Grammar Girl says,* "*Watch out,*"' as the arrow was coming toward me."

Single quotation marks are also sometimes used in headlines in place of double quotation marks.

'High School Musical' Gets a New Cast

Smith's Bad Attitude 'Unhelpful,' Says Jones

"And thus endeth the quotation marks section," quoth I.

3-29 # PARENTHESES

Parentheses are beautiful; I think of them as bookends for fun little statements. The words inside parentheses are called parenthetical elements, and they often act as asides. (See section 2-19; parenthetical expressions don't always need to be inside parentheses.) They are things you don't need to say but want to say anyway. They can clarify, direct, or give a sense of the writer's frame of mind.

Everyone loved Scott Sigler's new book (*Contagious*).

I'm fantasizing (just fantasizing, mind you) about skipping town and taking a job as a juggler.

Also see the chapters on snails (pp. 100–108) and aardvarks (pp. 95–96).

PARENTHESES WITH OTHER PUNCTUATION MARKS

3-30

If the parenthetical element is a complete sentence, the terminal punctuation goes inside the parenthesis.

Squiggly had many allergy symptoms. (He was itching, sneezing, and coughing.)

If the parenthetical element is not a complete sentence but comes at the end of a sentence, the terminal punctuation goes outside the parenthesis.

Squiggly had many allergy symptoms (itching, sneezing, and coughing).

If you have a complete sentence inside parentheses, and it falls inside another complete sentence, don't capitalize the first letter of the parenthetical sentence and don't use terminal punctuation unless the sentence requires a question mark or exclamation point.

Squiggly loves (we mean he truly adores them) fish.
Squiggly loves (should we say adores?) fish.

If the parenthetical element comes at the end of a clause or phrase that needs a comma, place the parenthetical comment before the comma.

When they scare me silly (and they usually do), haunted houses are my favorite exhibits at amusement parks.

3-31 BRACKETS

Brackets are most often used to insert editorial notes into a document.

> When they scare me silly, haunted houses are my favorite exhibits [Is "exhibits" the right word?—Ed.] at amusement parks.

Occasionally, brackets are also used when you need to make a parenthetical statement in a section that is already in parentheses—sort of how single quotation marks are used within double quotation marks. In general, you should avoid such multiple layers of asides.

> Squiggly loves (should we say adores? [do we even need to bother emphasizing this?]) fish.

UNDERLINING AND ITALICS

Most style guides recommend italics for titles of newspapers, movies, books, and plays. In the past, you had a choice between underlining and italics (as long as you were consistent—do you get tired of hearing me say that?), but now with websites and e-mail addresses automatically underlined by people's computers, italics is the safer way to go.

> Last week in New York, Squiggly saw *Mamma Mia!* and *Othello*. He found discounts advertised through the *New York Times*.

See Appendix section A-1 for more discussion of when to capitalize the word *the* in a title.

When you're mentioning short poems, articles, chapter titles, and names of songs, put quotation marks around these smaller works.

> I read the article "Squiggly Sees the City" in the *New York Times*.

Italics, underlining, or quotation marks can be used when you want to mark a specific word in the sentence—when you are actually writing about that word instead of using it for its meaning.

> If you look at the word "ugly" too long, it starts looking ugly.

Italics are also used when you put foreign words in your writing.

> The level of *schadenfreude* was embarrassing.

A note on style: you should almost never use italics, boldface, capital letters, or underlining to stress a word or phrase. Experts will call you lazy! If you don't think your point is standing out enough without these cheap font tricks, rewrite your sentence.

APOSTROPHE

I saved the apostrophe for the end of the chapter because it is, hands down, the most troublesome punctuation mark.

The apostrophe has two main uses in the English language: standing in for something that's missing and making a word possessive.

OMIT THIS!

Apostrophes first showed up in the 1500s as a way to indicate omissions. Today, the most common place to find this kind of apostrophe is in contractions, such as *can't* (for *cannot*), *that's* (for *that is*), and *it's* (for *it is* or *it has*).

Apostrophes can also be used in fun ways. If you're writing fiction, you can replace letters with apostrophes to reflect a character's dialect; for example, you could write "I saw 'em talkin' yonder" to indicate that the speaker said *'em* instead of *them* and *talkin'* instead of *talking*.

If you want to abbreviate the year, use an apostrophe to replace the first two numbers.

> What are your plans for '11?

If you want to refer to a whole decade—perhaps you want to write about the sixties—you write *'60s* with an apostrophe replacing the *19* and an *s* at the end.

> I wish I had lived in the '60s. (And you don't need an apostrophe before that final *s*; more on this later.)

The Plural of a Single Letter

How do you make a single letter plural, as in *Mind your* p's *and* q's? It's shocking, but you actually use an apostrophe before the *s*!

The apostrophe makes it clear that you're writing about multiple *p*'s and *q*'s. The apostrophe is especially important when you are writing about *a*'s, *i*'s, and *u*'s because without the apostrophe, readers could easily think you are writing the words *as*, *is*, and *us*.

FORMING POSSESSIVES: MINE, ALL MINE

How do you show ownership—that something belongs to someone? The basic rule is to add an apostrophe and *s*. Do so, and you've created a possessive (remember possessive pronouns from section 1-14?).

Aardvark's pencil

The apostrophe and *s* at the end of *Aardvark* means that the pencil belongs to Aardvark. It does not mean the plural of Aardvark, and it does not mean "Aardvark is pencil."

Singular Words That End with S

Many people are surprised to learn that there are two ways to make singular words that end with *s* possessive. Is it *Kansas's corn*, with an apostrophe and *s*, or *Kansas' corn*, with just an apostrophe at the end? Is it *James's reign* or *James' reign*?

Which is right? It turns out both are. Some style books suggest leaving off the extra *s*, and others recommend adding the apostrophe and *s* to almost all singular words that end with *s*.

This is one of those style decisions that cause people to freak out. Make sure you know your teachers' preferences!

Except That . . .

Certain singular words that end in *s* never take an apostrophe to become possessive. These exceptions are words that end with an *s* that makes an "iz" sound—such as *Moses*—and ancient names, such as *Zeus*, *Venus*, *Osiris*, and *Jesus*. For these, just add the apostrophe at the end of the word (e.g., *Moses' tablets*).

So, our first tough issue—how to make words that end with *s* possessive—doesn't actually have an answer; it's a style choice and you can do it either way. Many people use the rule that if they pronounce the second *s*, they write it out; and if not, they leave it off. Nevertheless, I prefer to pick one style and stick with it—I leave off the final *s* because doing so looks cleaner.

Plural Words That End with S

I always feel bad when the answer is that there isn't an answer, so here's a situation that has a firm rule: if the word ending with *s* is plural, such as *pirates*, add an apostrophe at the end to make it possessive.

> The pirates' escape route was blocked.

Plural words that don't end with *s*, such as *children*, do take an apostrophe and *s* at the end for possession.

> Fortunately, the children's room had a hidden doorway.
> The women's hats blew away.

Making Abbreviations Possessive

Make abbreviations possessive by adding an apostrophe and *s* to the end.

> The FBI's files were missing.
> Squiggly went to the CIA's headquarters.

Compound Possession

If you're writing about possession and have two subjects, you have to decide whether the two people possess something together or separately.

> Squiggly and Aardvark's cats are black.

The rule is if the two people share something, you use one apostrophe and *s*. So if Squiggly and Aardvark have the same cats, it is correct to say *Squiggly and Aardvark's cats* (with only one apostrophe and *s* after the last noun).

On the other hand, if Squiggly and Aardvark have different cats, you would say

Squiggly's and Aardvark's cats are black.

The rule is if they each possess something different, they each get an apostrophe and *s*.

QUICK AND DIRTY TIP

To remember this rule, think about hair dryers. (They're shaped like apostrophes.) Imagine that two people are going on the same trip. If they're sharing a hotel room, they can share a hair dryer on the trip, so then they can share the apostrophe and *s* too (*Squiggly and Aardvark's hotel room*). But if they aren't sharing a room, they each need their own hair dryer, and they each need their own "apostrophe s" (*Squiggly's and Aardvark's hotel rooms*).

So an apostrophe and *s* is like a hair dryer: you don't need to bring two if you're sharing the same hotel room.

When one of the subjects is a pronoun, use the possessive pronoun. As a rule of politeness, put yourself last in a list of people.

Squiggly's and my tree is thriving.

Possessives of Family Names

As you learned in the earlier section, Singular Words That End with *S*, you could go to Bob Jones' house or Bob Jones's house—both are correct.

But what if Bob has a family? Bob, Amy, and their children are the Joneses. The possessive form of *Joneses* is *Joneses'*. If the Joneses invite people over for dinner, their invitation could read two different ways.

> Please come to the <u>Joneses'</u> house for dinner. (possessive)
> The <u>Joneses</u> invite you to dinner. (plural)

When Not to Use an Apostrophe

Don't use an apostrophe if you're using a possessive pronoun.

> Aardvark said the baseball was his's.
> (Thud! That's the sound of Grammar Girl fainting.)

> Aardvark said the baseball was his.
> (Grammar Girl has been revived, thank you.)

Don't use an apostrophe when you're writing about plural years.

> Squiggly was really into the 1960's. (wrong)
> Squiggly was really into the 1960s. (right)

The 1960s is a plural in this sentence, meaning all ten years. The 1960s don't own anything (and possession is about ownership).

You can use an apostrophe to make decades possessive.

> The 1960s' answers to the world's problems were love and peace.

> Most people don't use an apostrophe with numbers.
>
> He has two 19s in his Social Security number.

Possessives and Adjectives: How to Tell the Difference

Is it a writers' strike or writers strike? Does the strike belong to the writers? Or is the word *writers* an adjective that tells people what kind of strike is happening? If the word is possessive, we need an apostrophe, but if it's an adjective, we don't need an apostrophe.

I believe it's pretty clear that the writers don't own the strike and that the word *writers* tells us more about what kind of strike it is. So I'd leave out the apostrophe. On the other hand, I'd include the apostrophe in *homeowners' association*, at least when the homeowners actually own or control the association that manages their property.

Notice that the apostrophe is after the final *s* in *homeowners*. If you call it a *homeowner's association*, then you're talking about an association owned by one homeowner.

Here's an even trickier one: *farmers market*. The market is used by the farmers, populated by the farmers, but generally not owned by the farmers. It seems reasonable to conclude that you don't use an apostrophe because the word *farmers* is there to identify the type of market. It's an adjective.

However, there are credible people who firmly believe the apostrophe is required in *farmers market*, *writers strike*, and similar phrases. It's a contentious topic, and you may have to defend your choice to someone no matter which choice you make.

Double Dipping or the Double Possessive

You can also use the word *of* to show possession.

You could write *the King of France* or you could write *France's King*, which means the same thing (although it doesn't have the same rhythm to it). These are normal possessives—there's nothing double about them.

Double possessives occur when you use both ways at the same time, as in *a friend of Squiggly's*. You have an apostrophe and *s* plus an *of*.

Although such a double possessive is allowed, I prefer *Squiggly's friend* over *a friend of Squiggly's*. Why not just write, *I am Squiggly's friend*?

Here's another example. It definitely sounds odd to say "a car of Squiggly." On the other hand, "a car of Squiggly's" sounds perfectly fine (this is assuming he has lots of cars and you're pointing out one of them). However, "a car of Squiggly's" doesn't sound as natural to me as "one of Squiggly's cars."

Luckily, we have a rule to follow. When you're talking about inanimate objects being the possessors—objects that aren't alive, such as France—you can't use a double possessive. The only time you can use a double possessive is when the possessor is definite and human or animal.

For example, you can write *a friend of my uncle's* but not *a friend of the museum's*. You have to write *a friend of the museum* because the museum isn't human or definite.

It would be OK to write *He's a friend of a friend's*, but we've all heard the common expression *a friend of a friend*. That's an idiom, which just shows that English isn't consistent, but we knew that already.

If possible, try to avoid double possessives; they are messy. Instead of *a friend of Squiggly's*, write *Squiggly's friend*.

Except That . . .

The Useful Double Possessive Exception

Sometimes, a double possessive helps clarify your meaning.

For example, if you attempt to avoid the double possessive and write *This is Marie's portrait*, you end up with an ambiguous sentence that could mean you are looking at a portrait of Marie or a portrait that is owned by Marie.

If you mean Marie owns the portrait, then the double possessive makes it clear.

This is a portrait of Marie's.

On the other hand, if you mean it's an exact likeness of Marie, then you need to rewrite the sentence.

This is a portrait of Marie.

Another time you might need to use a double possessive is when you use a possessive pronoun such as *theirs*, *hers*, or *mine*. In fact, it's impossible to avoid using a double possessive in cases such as *She is a relative of his*. It sounds normal to write *He's a friend of mine*. (*Mine* is the possessive.) You could reword such sentences by saying *She is his relative*, *She is one of his relatives*, or simply *They are related*.

Double possessives might also be necessary if you're using *that*, *those*, *this*, or *these* in your possessive. For example, *Get the hat of Aardvark's* sounds a bit odd. *Get that hat of Aardvark's* sounds a lot more natural.

My advice? Use double possessives carefully. You might want to avoid them in formal writing and perhaps use only one possessive at a time if it sounds natural.

POP QUIZ

Choose the correct sentence.

1. Squigglys' aunts' birthdays were in February.
2. Squiggly's aunts' birthdays were in February.
3. Squiggly's aunt's birthdays were in February.

Answer: 2

Whenever you are using apostrophes, take a second and a third look to make sure you're doing it right. Do you want to make your noun possessive, are you making a contraction, or do you instead have the plural form of a noun that shouldn't include an apostrophe?

POP QUIZ

Choose the correct sentence.

1. A. Gerard can't wait to visit the U.S..
   B. Gerard can't wait to visit the U.S.

2. A. I wonder why Sir Fragalot can't make a sentence.
   B. I wonder why Sir Fragalot can't make a sentence?

3. A. She couldn't wait to make an antique, lace dress.
   B. She couldn't wait to make an antique lace dress.

4. A. Squiggly wanted ice cream but Aardvark said no.
   B. Squiggly wanted ice cream, but Aardvark said no.

5. A. We have to go home because it's getting dark.
   B. We have to go home, because it's getting dark.

6. A. Go home now, Mildred.
   B. Go home now Mildred.

7. A. Get a glass of water, Squiggly has fainted.
   B. Get a glass of water; Squiggly has fainted.

8. A. Aardvark has a cold; therefore, he can't go fishing.
   B. Aardvark has a cold, therefore, he can't go fishing.

9. A. Sir Fragalot said, "After the chase."
   B. Sir Fragalot said, "After the chase".

10. A. The Smith childrens mother was late.
    B. The Smith children's mother was late.

Answers: 1. B, 2. A, 3. B, 4. B, 5. A, 6. A, 7. B, 8. A, 9. A, 10. B

Chapter Four

Quick and Dirty Tips

CONGRATULATIONS! You've made it this far, mastering parts of speech, parts of sentences, and punctuation.

By now you've learned the truth: English is a crazy language. (I'm sure you could already tell.) It has a dark side. There are rules, but always exceptions to those rules. What's a person to do?

Certain words are just more difficult than others. This chapter is about **usage**, choosing the right word or phrase. It's something everyone generally expects you to pick up on your own, and it's the thing you're most likely to get skewered for if you screw up. (Life is so unfair!) For instance, I don't recall ever being taught the difference between *affect* and *effect*. I was just expected to know.

So, to help you, I've created a list of what I call dirty words. I've picked the most common words and situations that confuse people. When I can, I'll give you shortcuts or tricks (Quick and Dirty Tips) for remembering the correct usage.

Very cleverly, I listed the words in alphabetical order.

A VERSUS *AN*: IT'S AN HONOR AND A HELP

Remember the indefinite articles from section 1-29?

Because it's tricky, I must remind you that you can't automatically put *a* before a consonant or *an* before a vowel. Remember the real rule is *a* goes before words that start with a consonant sound, and *an* goes before words that start with a vowel sound.

The usual tricky letters are *h, o,* and *u* because these letters can sound like either a vowel or a consonant.

> Squiggly saw <u>an</u> owl.
> It was <u>a</u> one-trick pony.

ACCIDENT: *ON ACCIDENT* OR *BY ACCIDENT*

(See *Prepositions: English Is a Crazy Language* in this chapter.)

ADVICE VERSUS *ADVISE*: CAN YOU HELP ME?

The main difference between these two words is that *advice* is a noun and *advise* is a verb—the act of giving advice.

Advice is one of those vague nouns that isn't a solid thing you can look at; it's a concept. I remember that *advice* is a noun by noting that it ends with *ice,* which is a noun.

> When she advised me to drive with my eyes open,
> I listened to her advice and was able to see the other
> cars zooming straight at me.

AFFECT VERSUS *EFFECT*: I WOULD NEVER AFFECT INTEREST JUST FOR EFFECT

If you don't know the difference between *affect* and *effect,* don't worry—you're not alone. Most of the time, *affect* is a verb and *effect* is a noun.

Affect most commonly means "to influence" or "to change."

The fire <u>affected</u> Aardvark's feeling of safety.
The rain <u>affected</u> Squiggly's plans.

Affect can also mean, roughly, "to act in a way that you don't feel," as in

He <u>*affected*</u> an air of superiority.

Effect has a lot of subtle meanings as a noun, but to me the meaning "a result" seems to be at the core of most of the definitions.

The <u>effect</u> was eye-popping.
The sound <u>effects</u> were amazing.
The rain had no <u>effect</u> on Squiggly's plans.

So most of the time *affect* is a verb and *effect* is a noun. There are rare instances where the roles are switched (see below), but if you stick with the verb-noun rule, you'll be right most of the time.

 ## Check It Out

Because *effect* is usually a noun, you can usually put an article in front of it and the sentence will still make sense.

The effect was eye-popping.
He kissed her for [*the*] effect.

Although *the* isn't necessary in the second example, it doesn't ruin the sentence.

On the other hand, look at these sentences where *affect* is a verb:

> The eye-popping arrow [*the*] affects everyone that way.
>
> The kiss [*the*] affected her.

You can't insert the definite article, *the*, before *affect* in those sentences, which means you want to use the verb (*affect*), not the noun (*effect*).

Quick and Dirty Tip 1: I remember that *effect* is usually the noun because *the* ends with *e* and *effect* starts with *e*, so if I can insert *the* in front of *effect*, the two *e*'s butt up against each other.

> Th<u>e</u> effect was eye-popping.

Quick and Dirty Tip 2: I remember that *affect* is usually the verb because verbs mean action and *affect* starts with an *a*—just like the word *action*. ✓

Except That . . .

Affect can be used as a noun when you are talking about psychology. It means the mood that someone appears to have. For example, a doctor may say, "The patient displayed a happy *affect*." Psychologists find the word useful because they can never really know what someone is feeling. Technically, they can only know how someone appears to be feeling.

Effect can be used as a verb that essentially means "to bring about" or "to accomplish." For example, you could say, "Aardvark hoped to *effect* change in the burrow."

ALLUDE VERSUS *ELUDE*: ARE YOU REFERRING TO ME?

Allude and *elude* sound similar and share the same Latin root word, but they don't mean the same thing.

Allude means to refer to indirectly.

> Hoping for an invitation, Squiggly alluded to his availability for the Valentine's Day dance.

Elude means to avoid or evade. The Quick and Dirty Tip is to remember that *escape* and *elude* both start with the letter *e*.

> Aardvark eluded the girls who wanted to ask him to dance.

ALOT VERSUS *A LOT* VERSUS *ALLOT*: A LOT OF TROUBLE

The correct spelling is *a lot*—two words. The Quick and Dirty Tip that helps me to remember is that *alot* (one word) wouldn't be enough to describe *a lot* (two words) of something.

Alot is not a word.

A lot means "a large number."

Allot means "to parcel out."

ALRIGHT VERSUS *ALL RIGHT*: ALL IS RIGHT WITH THE WORLD

It is not all right to spell *all right* as one word.

Alright is what language experts call a "nonstandard" spelling, which in less fancy terms means people will think you're dumb if you write it that way.

A Quick and Dirty Tip is to think of the phrase "all is right" to remind you that they are separate words.

ALUMNA, ALUMNAE, ALUMNUS, AND *ALUMNI*: LATIN STRIKES AGAIN

A female graduate or former attendee is an *alumna*, and a group of them are *alumnae*. A male graduate or former attendee is an *alumnus*, and a group of them are *alumni*. *Alumni* is also the word for a mixed group, so if the homecoming stands are filled with male and female graduates, they are collectively called *alumni*. A Quick and

Dirty Tip is to imagine that the final *A* in *alumna* is capitalized and therefore shaped like a skirt.

AS VERSUS *LIKE*: WHAT I LIKE ABOUT YOU

If you want to see blood and guts, just walk into a room full of grammarians, plop into a comfy chair, and say, "It's *like* I'm sitting in my own living room." I dare you!

Traditionally, *like* is a preposition and *as* is a conjunction. Nevertheless, people have been using *like* as if it were a conjunction for at least a hundred years, and grammarians have been raging against that use for just as long.

Prepositions create relationships between words in a clause or phrase and are not usually followed by verbs (see section 1-30).

> Squiggly walked *through* the door.
> Aardvark was *in* the loft.

A conjunction connects words, phrases, and clauses (see section 1-35). An entire clause (including a verb) can follow a conjunction.

> Squiggly walked through the door *and* caught Aardvark in the loft.

Because *like* is officially a preposition, use *like* when no verb follows it.

> Squiggly throws like **a raccoon.**
> It acted just like **my computer.**

Notice that when I use *like*, the words that come after are generally simple. *A raccoon* and *my computer* are the objects of the preposition.

If the clause that comes next includes a verb, you should use *as*.

Squiggly throws as **if he were a raccoon**.
He acted just as **I would expect him to**.

Notice that when I use *as* the words that come after tend to be more complex.

My cousin looks like **Batman**.
It's as **if my cousin were Batman**.
My neighbor yelled like **a maniac**.
My neighbor yelled as though **he were a maniac**.

The Quick and Dirty Tip that helps me to remember is that *like* is the simpler word—and it is followed by simpler words. *As* sounds stuffier and is followed by a more complex clause that contains a verb.

My advice is don't use *like* as a conjunction, especially in writing, unless you want to earn the wrath of raging grammarians.

ASSUME VERSUS PRESUME: ASSUME NOTHING

If you assume something about someone, you're basing your information on nothing—no facts or proof, just your belief gathered from thin air.

Assuming the waiter would say no, Aardvark refused to ask him for another piece of pie.

But if you presume to know something about someone, that presumption is based on evidence or facts.

Squiggly presumed that Grammar Girl would flinch when she saw the word misspelled as *alot*.

ASSURE VERSUS ENSURE VERSUS INSURE: FEELING SAFE

Assure, *ensure*, and *insure* have the same underlying meaning, but each has a slightly different use.

Assure is the only one of the three words that means "to reassure someone or to promise."

> I <u>assure</u> you that the chocolate is fresh.

Ensure chiefly means "to make certain or to guarantee."

> The drink Ensure <u>ensures</u> that people get their vitamins.
> He must <u>ensure</u> that the effect is eye-popping.

Insure can be interchangeable with *ensure* in some cases, but it is easiest to keep these words straight by reserving *insure* for references to insurance.

> I need to <u>insure</u> my car.

Bad Dog

Because *bad* and *badly* are misused so much, I decided to repeat the rules here in a shortened form (see section 1-27).

The Quick and Dirty Tip is that it is correct to say you feel bad when you are expressing an emotion.

The correct sentence is *I feel bad* because you're using *feel* as a linking verb, so it needs an adjective (*bad*) instead of an adverb (*badly*). *Bad* is modifying the subject.

Don't feel bad if you've made this mistake. You're not alone. In fact, people may try to tell you you're wrong when you get it right. I'm Grammar Girl, and people even try to argue about this with me! Can you believe it? Don't give in; just remember about linking verbs and action verbs.

BECAUSE VERSUS *DUE TO*: BECAUSE THE MONEY WAS DUE TO HER

When you're choosing between *because of* and *due to*, *because of* is almost always the better choice. For example, it's best to say, "I don't have any homework this week *because of* [not due to] the holiday," and "*Because of* [not due to] the holiday, I don't have any homework this week."

It's best to reserve *due to* for times when you mean "owed" or "expected." For example, "He sent the money that was *due to* her," or "She was *due to* arrive at noon."

BECAUSE VERSUS *SINCE*: THE CAUSE OF THE MATTER

There is a distinction between *because* and *since*, but you'll notice that most people don't bother with it. In everyday use, it isn't a crime to use these words interchangeably, but if you don't want strict grammarians tsking at you, it's easy to figure out the proper way to use each word.

Since deals with time.

> Since my early podcasts, I've noticed that the number of people who write to me has grown.

The above example shows that something happened from the time I started my podcasts. The number of people who wrote grew from a starting point in time. The sentence doesn't say anything about the *reason* more people are writing to me.

Because deals with something that brings about a result or an effect.

> Because I know that language evolves, I usually accept changes in word usage.

Time doesn't enter into the second example.

The Quick and Dirty Tip is to remember that the word *cause* is within *because* and you use *because* when you want to show cause—that something happened because of something else.

BETWEEN VERSUS *AMONG*: CHOOSE BETWEEN THE BEES AND THE TWEENS

Use *between* when you are writing about two things and *among* when you are writing about more than two things. If you follow this guideline, you'll be right most of the time.

> Squiggly dreaded choosing between art and gym.

Between and *among* can also tell the reader different things about location or direction. Think about the difference between these two sentences:

> Squiggly walked between the trees.
> Squiggly walked among the trees.

Squiggly walked between the trees gives you the idea that he stayed on the path; he either walked between two trees or was on a route that was surrounded by trees. On the other hand, *Squiggly walked among the trees* gives you the idea that he wandered around

a park or forest. He may have had an endpoint in mind, but it doesn't sound as if he went from point A to point B on a defined path.

> ## Except That . . .
> Yup, we have an exception here.
>
> You can use the word *between* when you are talking about distinct, individual items, even if there are more than two of them. You would use *between* in this example because the three groups are negotiating individually: *The negotiations between the cheerleaders, the dance squad, and the flag team were going well despite the confetti incident.*
>
> If you were talking about the groups collectively, you would use *among*: *The teacher divided the banners among the booster groups.*
>
> Use <u>between</u> when you're <u>being</u> specific about the items, and be prepared to be corrected even though you're right.

BIANNUAL VERSUS *SEMIANNUAL*
(See *Semiannual* Versus *Biannual*.)

BRING VERSUS *TAKE*: BRING IT ON
It's all about you.

Whether you use *bring* or *take* depends on your point of reference for the action. You ask people to bring things to the place you are, and you take things to some other place.

Don't you love it when grammar is all about you?

> I asked Aardvark to bring Squiggly to my party next week.

> Aardvark called Squiggly and asked, "May I take you to Grammar Girl's party?"

I am asking Aardvark to bring Squiggly because I am at the destination. From my perspective, Aardvark is bringing someone here. Aardvark is offering to take Squiggly because he is transporting Squiggly to a remote destination. From Aardvark's perspective, he is taking someone there.

The rule is that things are brought to the speaker and taken away from the speaker. You ask people to bring things to you, and you take things to other people. You ask people to bring you soda, and you offer to take the dishes to the kitchen. You tell people to bring you good news, and you take your camera to the beach.

Finally, an interesting note is that the words *come* and *go* follow rules that are similar to those for *bring* and *take*. *Come* is like *bring*: you ask people to come here—to come to where you are. And *go* is like *take*: you tell people to go away—to move away from your location.

> Aardvark and Squiggly are coming to my party.

> When Aardvark calls Squiggly, he'll say, "Let's go to Grammar Girl's party."

I suspect that one reason people get confused about *bring* and *take* is that there are many exceptions to the basic rules. For example, idioms such as *take a bath* and phrasal verbs such as *bring up*, *bring about*, *take down*, and *take after* don't follow the rules.

BY VERSUS *BYE*: BUH-BYE

By is a preposition, meaning near or beside. *Bye* is a shortened version of *good-bye.*

> Squiggly stood by Aardvark, waving bye to Grammar Girl as she began her ten-city book tour.

CAN VERSUS MAY: THE CAN-CAN DANCE

You've been there. You've done that.

How many of your teachers have responded "*May* I go to the bathroom!" when you've raised your hand and asked "*Can* I go to the bathroom"?

Technically, *can* is used to ask if something is possible, and *may* is used to ask if something is permissible.

So yes, you're able to go to the bathroom (right?). What you need is your teacher's permission to proceed—to be allowed to leave the class and go to the bathroom.

Nevertheless, substituting *can* for *may* is done so commonly it can hardly be considered wrong. Use *may* when you are in formal situations or want to be especially proper, but don't get too hung up about it in everyday life (unless, of course, your English teacher will let you go only if you ask correctly).

CAPITAL VERSUS CAPITOL: A CAPITAL IDEA

The noun *capitol* refers to state capitol buildings or the Capitol building in Washington, DC.

Quick and Dirty Tip: You can remember that the rotunda of the Capitol building in Washington, DC, is round like the letter *o*.

Capital refers to

- uppercase letters (use *capital* letters)
- wealth (the bank needs to raise *capital*)
- the death penalty (*capital* punishment)
- something important (a *capital* idea)
- a city that is the seat of government for its region or is important in some way (Carson City is the *capital* of Nevada)

Don't get confused by the fact that *capital* with an *al* is used for a capital city and *capitol* with an *ol* is used for a state's capitol building. Just remember the O-shaped rotunda. (See Appendix section A-1 for when to capitalize *capitol*.)

CITE VERSUS *SITE* VERSUS *SIGHT*: HOW UNSIGHTLY

Cite is an important word to know for writing papers. When you quote people, you are citing their work. It may help to remember that *cite* and *citation* have the same root.

> Grammar Girl <u>cited</u> other grammarians' work in her latest book.

Site is a location or place, such as a work site or website.

> Grammar Girl calls the coffee house her work <u>site</u>.
> <u>Site</u> the house on the lot.

Sight refers to the ability to see.

> Grammar Girl caught <u>sight</u> of Squiggly across the street.
> The old wizard was losing his <u>sight</u>.

COME VERSUS *GO*

(See *Bring* Versus *Take*.)

COMPLIMENT VERSUS *COMPLEMENT*: YOU LOOK FABULOUS

I have a great memory trick for remembering the difference between *compliment* and *complement*. A compliment (with an *i*) is a word of praise, so just remember the sentence

> <u>I</u> like to give compl<u>i</u>ments.

Complement (with an *e*) means that something pairs well with something else. You can remember the meaning by thinking things that complement each other often complete each other, and *complement* and *complete* both have two e's in them.

Things that complem̲e̲nt each other often
complet̲e̲ each other.

Blue and orange are complementary colors.

The full complement of players showed up for the game.

CONNOTE VERSUS *DENOTE*: THE CONNOTATIONS WERE SHOCKING

Even Grammar Girl has a hard time keeping *connote* and *denote* straight. *To connote* means to suggest or imply something beyond the actual meaning.

In some circles, *geek* connotes brains and coolness; in other circles, *geek* connotes loser.

Denote indicates that there is no question about the connection; the connection is explicit.

Squiggly's party hat denoted his excitement for the event.

COULD CARE LESS VERSUS *COULDN'T CARE LESS*: DO YOU CARE?

If you say you "could care less," you're not saying what you really mean. *I could care less* is used so often that some people consider it an idiom, but many people find it annoying. The correct statement is *I couldn't care less*.

I could care less whether I speak English correctly.
(Wrong. In other words, it's possible for me to care even less than I do. I still have some reserves of caring left.)

I couldn't care less whether I speak English correctly.
(Right. This means it isn't possible for me to care any less than I do. I have no reserves of caring left. It

would be a sad statement to make, but it's worded properly.)

DECEPTIVELY: A WORD THAT SHOULD BE BANNED

If you write that a crossword puzzle is deceptively easy, does that mean it is easy or hard? It can actually mean either. Using the word *deceptively* can lead to confusion, and the best approach is to rewrite the sentence to avoid it.

DESPITE VERSUS IN SPITE OF: SPITEFUL GRAMMAR

In spite of and *despite* mean the same thing and are interchangeable. For example, it is correct to say either of the following:

She ran well, despite having old shoes.
She ran well, in spite of having old shoes.

Some people prefer *despite* because it is shorter.

Despite the fact that you can choose which word to use, you cannot mix the two. To write *in despite of* is wrong.

DIFFERENT FROM VERSUS DIFFERENT THAN: WHAT'S THE DIFF?

Different from is preferred to *different than*. The Quick and Dirty Tip? *Different* has two *f*'s and only one *t,* so the better choice between *than* and *from* is usually the one that starts with an *f.*

Squiggly knew he was di__f__f__erent __f__rom the other snails.

DISINTERESTED VERSUS UNINTERESTED: I DON'T CARE

The English language is not always logical or friendly. Here we have two words that should mean the same thing but, of course, don't.

A *disinterested* person has no preconceived ideas or opinions about something.

A judge should be disinterested, listening to a case with an open mind and no preformed opinions.

Someone who is *uninterested* just doesn't care; the person's curiosity is not stimulated.

Squiggly was so uninterested he had to hold back his yawns when Grammar Girl explained the different verb tenses.

DRAGGED VERSUS DRUG: JUST SAY NO TO DRUG

Dragged is the proper past tense of the verb *to drag* when you're talking about pulling something across the floor. The only standard meaning of *drug* has to do with pharmaceuticals or illegal drugs. The Quick and Dirty Tip is to just say no to *drug*.

Aardvark dragged Squiggly out of bed.

EACH AND EVERY: I WANT EACH OF YOU TO WIN

Each and *every* mean the same thing and are considered singular nouns, so they take singular verbs. (Note the singular verbs in the following examples.) If you want to get technical, you can use *each* to highlight the individual items or people.

Each car is handled with care.

Use *every* to highlight the larger group.

Every car has airbags these days.

People often say "each and every" for emphasis, but in most cases it is redundant.

EFFECT VERSUS AFFECT

(See *Affect* Versus *Effect*.)

E.G. VERSUS *I.E.*

E.g. and *i.e.* are both abbreviations for Latin terms. While *i.e.* stands for *id est* and means "that is," *e.g.* stands for *exempli gratia*, which means roughly "for example."

> Aardvark likes card games, e.g., bridge and crazy eights.
> Squiggly visited Ivy League colleges, e.g., Harvard and Yale.
> Aardvark doesn't have any plans, i.e., he's available.

I always put a comma after *e.g.* and *i.e.* My computer spell-checker freaks out and wants me to remove the comma, but five out of six style guides surveyed recommend using the comma.

ELUDE VERSUS *ALLUDE*

(See *Allude* Versus *Elude*.)

EVERYONE VERSUS *EVERYBODY*: EVERYONE LOVES SQUIGGLY

Everyone and *everybody* mean the same thing: every person. You can use them interchangeably, and they are considered singular.

> Everyone loves Squiggly.
> Everybody is coming over after the parade.

FARTHER VERSUS *FURTHER*: FARTHER THAN YOU'VE EVER GONE BEFORE

Farther refers to physical distance, and *further* deals with metaphorical or figurative distance. The Quick and Dirty Tip is easy. *Far* obviously relates to physical distance, and it's in the word *farther*.

> Squiggly and Aardvark walked to a town far, far away. After many miles, Squiggly grew tired. "How much farther?" he asked in despair.

Squiggly used *farther* because he was asking about physical distance.

> Aardvark, frustrated with Squiggly, said, "I'm tired of your complaining; <u>further</u>, I'm tired of carrying your maracas."

In this case, Aardvark used *further* because he isn't talking about physical distance, he's talking about metaphorical distance: further along the list of irritations. The phrases *moreover* or *in addition* can be substituted for *further*.

Sometimes the Quick and Dirty Tip breaks down because it's hard to decide whether you're talking about physical distance. For example, take a look at this sentence:

> I'm further along in my book than you are in yours.

You could think of it as a physical distance through the pages and use *farther* or as a figurative distance through the story and use *further*.

The good news is that in these ambiguous cases it doesn't matter which word you choose. It's fine to use *further* and *farther* interchangeably when the distinction isn't clear.

FEMALE VERSUS *WOMAN*: I AM WOMAN, HEAR ME ROAR

When do you use *female*, and when do you use *woman*?

The word *woman* is primarily a noun, but it is also sometimes used as an adjective. *Female* is primarily used as an adjective, but it is sometimes also used as a noun, especially in scientific settings.

A Quick and Dirty Tip for testing the validity of using *woman* as an adjective in a particular sentence is to substitute the word *man* to see if it makes sense. One day I hope that we'll have progressed so far that we don't need to use the word *man* as a test.

For example, it sounds ridiculous to say someone is "the first man Speaker of the House." Of course, you would say "male Speaker of the House."

Therefore, even though it's not strictly wrong to use *woman* as an adjective, it's better to use the primary adjective, *female*, and say that Nancy Pelosi was the first female Speaker of the House and Sarah Palin was the first female Republican vice presidential nominee.

FEWER VERSUS *LESS*: IF THERE WERE FEWER GRAMMARIANS...

Fewer and *less* are easy to mix up. They mean the same thing—the opposite of *more*—but you use them in different circumstances. The rule is to use *fewer* with **count nouns** and *less* with **mass nouns.**

It's easy to remember the difference between count nouns and mass nouns.

A count noun is just something you can count. On my desk I see books, pens, and M&Ms. I can count all those things, so they are count nouns and the right word to use is *fewer.* There are more letters in *fewer* than in *less*, so you can remember that there are more things to count.

> I should eat <u>fewer</u> M&Ms.

Mass nouns are just things you can't count individually. Again, on my desk I see clutter and tape. Those things can't be counted individually, so the right word to use is *less.*

> If I had <u>less</u> clutter, my desk would be cleaner.

Another clue is that you don't make mass nouns plural: I would never say I have clutters on my desk or I need more tapes to hold my book covers together.

Except That . . .

There are exceptions to the rule that *less* is only for things you can't count. For example, although you can count time, money, and distance, they can also be divided into infinitely small units, which makes them more like mass nouns, so you use the word *less*.

> **The reception lasted <u>less</u> than two hours.**
> **I hope the band charged <u>less</u> than $400.**
> **The gas station was <u>less</u> than three miles away.**

Remember that although time, money, and distance are different, if you stick with the rule that *less* is for mass nouns and *fewer* is for count nouns, you'll be right most of the time.

FLAMMABLE VERSUS *INFLAMMABLE*: BURN, BABY, BURN

Flammable means that something is capable of burning easily. *Inflammable* means the same thing, but many people mistakenly believe that it means resistant to burning.

Inflammable is a lot like *deceptively* (see that entry in this chapter): If you use the word, your meaning will be unclear to some of your readers. Therefore, it's best to avoid *inflammable*. The famous usage expert Bryan Garner calls such words, which have become so muddled that we should avoid them, "skunked terms."

GOES VERSUS *SAYS*: ARE YOU TALKING TO ME?

You shouldn't use *goes* to introduce dialogue.

> Aardvark goes, "You mean I'm wrong?"
> (Yes, Aardvark, it's wrong to use *goes* to mean *says*.)

> Aardvark says, "I now know which word to use when I mean that someone is talking."
> (Grammar Girl is so much happier now!)

GOOD VERSUS *WELL*: HOW YOU DOIN'?

Well is usually an adverb (it modifies verbs), and *good* is usually an adjective (it modifies nouns). Therefore, when you're dealing with action verbs such as *run*, *swim*, and *play*, you modify them with the adverb—*well*.

> Sir Fragalot fences <u>well</u>.
> Squiggly swam <u>well</u> at the meet today.

You use the adjective *good* when you're modifying nouns.

> Sir Fragalot did a <u>good</u> job at the fencing match.
> Squiggly got a <u>good</u> time in the swim meet today.

(See section 1-27 for more about *good* and *well*.)

GOODNESS GRACIOUS!

What happens if you're feeling healthier today than you were yesterday?

> I feel better than I did yesterday.
> (Grammar Girl is so happy to hear that.)

> I feel gooder than I did yesterday.
> (Grammar Girl feels a faint coming on and doesn't care how you feel!)

The correct comparison words are *good*, *better*, and *best* (not *good*, *gooder*, and *goodest*).

> Aardvark is a good piano player.
> Aardvark is a <u>better</u> piano player than Squiggly.
> (comparing two things)

> Compared to Aardvark and Squiggly, Grammar
> Girl is the <u>best</u> piano player because she can
> reach the keys and pedals.
>
> (comparing three things)

See section 1-28 for more on comparatives and super-latives.

The same is true for bad—*bad*, *worse*, and *worst* are correct. Never use *bad, badder, baddest*. Writing *baddest* would be the worst thing, indeed!

Quick and Dirty Tip: I used to have a hard time remembering that *worse* is the correct word for comparing two things and *worst* needs three or more objects. My solution? *Worse* ends in an *e*, and *worst* ends in a *t*. So notice that in the alphabet, *e* comes before *t*. *Worse* is used for two things (two comes before three), and *worst* is used for three or more things.

GRADUATED VERSUS *GRADUATED FROM*: LET'S GET THOSE KIDS GRADUATED

Although the *graduated high school* construction is becoming more common, it is incorrect.

A school does the act of graduating a student.

> Stanford graduated thousands of students this year.

Students are graduated from a school.

> Squiggly graduated from Stanford.

If you're going to graduate, do it correctly. Graduate *from* school with A's in English.

GRAY VERSUS *GREY*: EARL GREY IS MY HERO

Have you ever wondered why *gray* is spelled two ways? *Grey* is the preferred spelling in Britain, whereas *gray* is more popular in America. You can remember the difference by thinking that the *a* in *gray* is for *American*.

HANGED VERSUS *HUNG*: WELL, I'LL BE HANGED

There are two different versions of the past tense of the verb *hang*. You say curtains were hung and people were hanged. You can remember that by thinking of the poem that begins *'Twas the Night Before Christmas*: "The stockings were hung by the chimney with care." That's right. Stockings were hung.

On the other hand, use *hanged* when you are talking about killing people by dangling them from a rope. I remember this by thinking that hangings were common in the Wild West, and I imagine a prospector expressing surprise by saying, "I'll be hanged!"

HISTORIC VERSUS *HISTORICAL*: DON'T GET HYSTERICAL

Historic and *historical* are both adjectives, but they have different meanings.

Historic means something important or influential in history.

> Historic events include the first moon walk, the signing of the Declaration of Independence, and the invention of the printing press.

It would be incorrect to say "We sell historic lanterns," unless the lanterns are important to history (maybe if Paul Revere had owned them, they would be historic lanterns). Historic treaties, historic houses, and historic battlefields were important or famous things in history.

Historical, on the other hand, refers to anything from the past, important or not.

> Historical events include previous annual meetings at the United Nations, baseball games, and graduation ceremonies.

This happened in the past, but it wasn't an earth-shaking event. A historical occasion would be just some occasion in the past, not necessarily an important one. Historical documents are just documents that record the past.

You've probably read a historical novel, perhaps a historical romance; books in these genres are set in the past. There is nothing especially important about these books; if there were, they'd be historic books. The Gutenberg Bible is a historic book, for example, because it was a major work, starting the age of the printed book. Thank you, Mr. Gutenberg!

It's common for people to mix up these two words. A Quick and Dirty Tip to help you keep them straight is to think that *ic* is important, and they both start with *i*; and *al* is all in the past, and those both start with *a*.

Remember, you're pronouncing the *h* in *historic* and *historical*, so use *a* in front of both these words. (See section 1-29 for more on *a* versus *an*.)

To sum up, something historic is important whereas something historical is all in the past, and it's better to say *a historic* than *an historic*.

HOWEVER: CAN YOU START A SENTENCE WITH IT?

You might ask what this entry is doing here. The answer is that I felt you needed to know about adverbs, commas, semicolons, conjunctions—pretty much everything—before we could tackle whether it is correct to start a sentence with *however*.

Who knew that a single word would need so much knowledge?

When people ask me about sentence-starting rules, *however* is the word they mention most often. It's fine to use *however* at the beginning of a sentence; you just need to know when to use a comma.

The comma is important because *however* is a conjunctive adverb that can be used in two different ways: it can be a conjunction that joins main clauses, or it can be an adverb that modifies a clause.

Adverbs modify clauses and whole sentences. Remember how "verbishly" active they are! A conjunctive adverb is a transitional word that joins two clauses that could be independent sentences, and it provides meaning about the relationship between the two sentences. Examples include *however, therefore,* and *nevertheless.* (See Appendix section A-2 for more examples.)

If you start a sentence with *however* and don't follow it with a comma, *however* means "in whatever manner" or "to whatever extent."

> <u>However</u> Squiggly tried, he couldn't get his mind off chocolate.

However isn't acting like a conjunction. It's not joining anything to anything else. It's behaving like an adverb, which everyone thinks is fine.

On the other hand, some grammarians believe that you should not start a sentence with *however* when you mean "nevertheless" or "on the other hand." Brace yourself. I'm going to dis them (I'm rarely so brave, but I have a strong opinion about this rule).

When you put a comma after *however* at the beginning of a sentence, everyone knows it means "nevertheless." There's no reason to outlaw a perfectly reasonable use of the word when you can solve the problem with a comma!

> Squiggly couldn't forget about chocolate. <u>However,</u> he wasn't trying very hard.

> Squiggly was Aardvark's best friend. <u>However,</u> sometimes Aardvark found him exasperating.

If you're afraid of those grammarians who believe starting a sentence with the conjunction *however* is evil and wrong and you want to avoid their ire, it's not hard to do—you can substitute the word *nevertheless* or grab a semicolon and use it to connect your two main clauses instead of separating them with a period.

> Squiggly was Aardvark's best friend. <u>Nevertheless,</u> sometimes Aardvark found him exasperating.

> Squiggly was Aardvark's best friend; <u>however,</u> sometimes Aardvark found him exasperating.

Treat the other conjunctive adverbs the same way.

> Squiggly was Aardvark's best friend; <u>indeed,</u> sometimes Aardvark thought Squiggly was his only friend.

You can also bury a *however* that means "nevertheless" in the middle of a sentence if it makes sense with the rhythm of your sentence. When you put *however* in the middle of a sentence, it should be surrounded by commas.

> Friendship, <u>however,</u> is a complicated dance.

> A gift of chocolate, <u>however,</u> has the power to salve minor missteps.

People often get confused about this point because in long sentences sometimes you need a comma and sometimes you need a semicolon with your *however*. Just remember that you use the semicolon (the sentence splicer) only when you are joining two main clauses and the *however* just happens to be in the way, shouting "nevertheless."

Don't let anyone tell you it's wrong to start a sentence with *however*. Mind your commas and semicolons, and don't use any punctuation after *however* when you use it to mean "in whatever manner" or "to whatever extent."

Whew.

I.E. VERSUS *E.G.*
(See *E.g.* Versus *I.e.*)

IF VERSUS *WHETHER*: IT ALL DEPENDS ON THE CONDITIONS

In informal writing and speech *if* and *whether* are often used interchangeably, but in formal writing, it's a good idea to make a distinction between them because the meaning can sometimes be different depending on which word you use.

The formal rule is to use *if* when you have a conditional sentence and *whether* when you are showing that two alternatives are possible.

Here's an example where the two words could be interchangeable:

Squiggly didn't know <u>whether</u> Aardvark would arrive on Friday.

Squiggly didn't know <u>if</u> Aardvark would arrive on Friday.

In either sentence the meaning is that Aardvark may or may not arrive on Friday.

But check out this next sentence—the words are not interchangeable:

Squiggly didn't know <u>whether</u> Aardvark would arrive on Friday or Saturday.

Because I used *whether*, you know that there are two

possibilities: Aardvark will arrive on Friday, or Aardvark will arrive on Saturday.

Now see how the sentence has a different meaning when I use *if* instead of **whether**:

> Squiggly didn't know <u>if</u> Aardvark would arrive on Friday or Saturday.

Now, in addition to arriving on Friday or Saturday, there is the possibility that Aardvark may not arrive at all. That's why it is best to use **whether** when you have two possibilities, even when the meaning wouldn't change if you use *if*. It's safer and more consistent.

Here's a final pair of examples:

> Call Squiggly <u>if</u> you are going to arrive on Friday.

> Call Squiggly <u>whether</u> or not you are going to arrive on Friday.

The first sentence is conditional. *Call Squiggly if you are going to arrive on Friday* means Aardvark is expected to call only if he is coming.

The second sentence is not conditional. *Call Squiggly whether or not you are going to arrive on Friday* means Aardvark is expected to call either way.

In summary, use **whether** when you have two choices, and use *if* for conditional sentences.

Whether Versus *Whether or Not*

When do you need *or not* after **whether**? Why did I say, "Call Squiggly whether *or not* you are going to arrive on Friday"? Often the *or not* is just extra fluff and should be left off.

> Squiggly didn't know <u>whether or not</u> Aardvark would arrive on Friday.

> Squiggly didn't know <u>whether</u> Aardvark
> would arrive on Friday.

In the above example, adding *or not* didn't change the meaning or emphasis. I would leave it out.

On the other hand, you need the full phrase **whether or not** when you mean "regardless of whether." It shows that there is equal emphasis on both options.

> Call Squiggly <u>regardless of whether</u>
> you are going to arrive on Friday.

> Call Squiggly <u>whether or not</u> you are
> going to arrive on Friday.

IN SPITE OF VERSUS *DESPITE*
(See *Despite* Versus *In Spite Of*)

INTO VERSUS *IN TO* VERSUS *IN*: INTO THE WILD
I'm going to tackle this one in parts. First, *in* versus *into*.

When you use *in*, you're indicating position.

> Her iPod was <u>in</u> her pocket.

When you use *into* in a sentence, you're indicating movement; an action is happening.

> She stuffed her iPod <u>into</u> her backpack.

Now, on to comparing *into* and *in to*.

Into is a preposition that has many definitions, but as I just said, they all generally relate to direction and motion.

On the other hand, *in* by itself can be an adverb, a preposition, or an adjective. *To* by itself is a preposition or an adverb or part of an infinitive (see section 1-11), such as *to fly*. Sometimes *in* and *to* just end up next to each other.

Examples will help!

He walked *into* the room.

(In which direction was he going? Into the room. There's motion; *into* is a preposition.)

We broke *in to* the room.

(*Broke in* is a phrasal verb. The word *in* belongs with *broke*. The word *to* is a preposition that points readers to the location of the break-in—the room.)

Squiggly walked *into* the lamppost by accident.

(*Into* is a preposition showing motion and direction.)

Squiggly walked *in to* hear Aardvark talking about the surprise party.

(Because *to* is part of the verb *hear* [*to hear*, an infinitive], keep it separate from *in*.)

"Come *into* the house now!"

(*Into* indicates movement, and it is a preposition.)

"Ask your brother to come *in to* dinner."

(*Come in* is a phrasal verb, and dinner is what he's coming to.)

IT'S VERSUS ITS: IT'S HORRIBLE

When I was in second grade, I lost a spelling bee because I misspelled the word *its*. I put an apostrophe in when I shouldn't have, and it was a very traumatic moment for me. It's now my calling to save all of you from similar apostrophe-induced horrors.

It's with an apostrophe and *s* always means "it is" or "it has." *It's* is a contraction of two words: *it is* or *it has*.

> It's [it is] lunchtime.
> It's [it is] a shame the chocolate tree is out of season.
> It's [it has] been a long time since we saw Joe.

Its is the possessive form of *it*, just like *hers*, *ours*, and *yours*. None of the possessive pronouns take an apostrophe *s* to become possessive.

> The tree needs <u>its</u> branches trimmed.
> The chocolate tree has a scratch on <u>its</u> trunk.

The reason for the confusing *its* trap is that you make most nouns possessive by adding an apostrophe and *s* to the end, but not pronouns.

Just remember to take an extra second to consider whether you are using the right form. Even if you know the difference, it's easy to slip up when you are writing quickly.

Contraction Confusion Continues

It's easy to confuse *who's* and *whose, you're* and *your,* and *they're* and *their.*

> <u>Who's</u> at the door? (a contraction of *who is*)
>
> <u>Whose</u> hat are you wearing? (a possessive pronoun)
>
> <u>You're</u> my favorite grammarian. (a contraction of *you are*)
>
> <u>Your</u> interest in the many wonders of the comma intrigues me. (a possessive pronoun)

LAY VERSUS LIE

You need to have patience for *lay* and *lie*. Figuring out how to use them isn't quick, but it's definitely dirty.

Subject Versus Object

Before you can choose between *lay* and *lie*, you have to determine whether you are talking about the subject or object of a sentence. You remember the difference, right? (You read about it in sections 2-1 and 2-3.)

Just to make it easier, we'll review it here.

The subjects of a sentence are the people or things doing something, and the objects of the sentence are having something done to them.

Take the sentence *I love you*. *I* is the subject. You are the object of my affection, and *you* is also the object of the sentence. How's that? You are the object of my affection and the object of my sentence. It's like a Valentine's Day card and a grammar trick all rolled into one.

Now that we have that embarrassing love stuff behind us, we can move on.

Don't Lay an Egg

If you forget about the *lie* that means "to tell an untruth" and just focus on the setting/reclining meaning of *lay* and *lie*, then the important distinction is that *lay* requires an object (technically, it's called a **direct object**) and *lie* does not.

You *lie* on the sofa because you are taking an action (and there is no direct object), but you *lay* the book on the table because *lay* refers to the book, which is the target of your action (making the book the direct object).

These examples are in the present tense:

<u>Lie</u> down on the sofa!
<u>Lay</u> down your pencil!

Your pencil is the direct object.

QUICK AND DIRTY TIP

Everyone knows that hens lay eggs. Because *eggs* is the object of the sentence, you can always remember that *lay* needs an object. Another way to remember is to think of the line "Hens lie down to lay eggs."

Conjugating *Lay* and *Lie*: I'm Getting Tense

Now that you know which verb to use when you're dealing with the present tense, I'm going to make things more confusing by dealing with the past and the future. Remember that I said English is crazy? Well, it's about to make *you* crazy.

Lay is also the past tense of *lie*. (Don't hate me!)

Present Tense	Past Tense	Present Participle	Past Participle
lay	laid	laying	have laid
lie	lay	lying	have lain

This is what it would look like in all the tenses:

	Lie (no object)	**Lay** (needs an object)
Present Tense	Squiggly wants to lie down.	Aardvark wants to lay the book on the table.
Past Tense	Last week Squiggly lay down on the floor.	Aardvark laid the book on the table.

	Lie (no object)	**Lay** (needs an object)
Present Participle	Squiggly is lying on the floor.	Aardvark is laying the book on the table.
Past Participle	Squiggly has lain on the floor for days.	Aardvark has laid the book on the table.

Don't feel bad if you can't remember these verb forms right away. Practice will help, and truthfully, I still have to look up most of them every time I use them. It's important to know what you know and to look up what you don't know because these *are* hard-and-fast rules.

Pop Homework Assignment

Check out the classic rock songs "Lay, Lady, Lay" by Bob Dylan and "Lay Down Sally" by Eric Clapton. Sure, they're old, but they're great. Unfortunately, neither Dylan nor Clapton had Grammar Girl to help him. If either had, the songs would have been grammatically correct—"Lie, Lady, Lie" and "Lie Down Sally"—but would the lyrics have been as catchy?

LEND VERSUS *LOAN*: LEND ME YOUR EARS

In Britain, *lend* is the verb and *loan* is the noun. A Quick and Dirty Tip is to remember that *loan* and *noun* both have o's in them, and *lend* and *verb* both have e's in them.

In the United States, most language experts consider the words interchangeable when you are talking about money or items. Nevertheless, some sticklers disagree, and if you wish to avoid their ire, you should stick to the British rules.

Squiggly asked Aardvark to lend him money and a bike.

Aardvark gave Squiggly a <u>loan</u> of money but wouldn't <u>lend</u> his bike.

Aardvark was usually happy to <u>lend</u> a hand, but even friendship has its limits.

LESS VERSUS *FEWER*
(See *Fewer* Versus *Less*.)

LET'S: LET'S NOT!
The apostrophe in *let's* indicates a contraction—something removed—not ownership. *Let's* really means *let us* (the *u* in *us* is missing).

Let's go! = Let us go!

(Grammar Girl is now humming "Let's Go" by The Cars.)

LIKE: LIKE, TOTALLY
You might use *like* and *you know* when speaking, but it's a definite no-no when writing. Words such as *like* and *you know* are fillers—they don't say anything.

Like, you know, it's, like, you know.

I'm so, you know, like, happy, you know, that, like, I can't, like, breathe.

Maybe, as you become conscious of how often you use these words, you will cut down on them when you're speaking. Not all at once. Take out two a day, then three. If you can do it, people will take you more seriously.

LIKE VERSUS *AS*
(See *As* Versus *Like*.)

LIT VERSUS *LIGHTED*: COME ON, BABY, LIGHT MY FIRE

Strange as it may seem, both *lit* and *lighted* are equally acceptable past tense forms of the verb *to light*.

Lighted is a regular form (because you add *ed* to the end to make it past tense), and *lit* is an irregular form (because you change the spelling instead of adding *ed* to the end), but irregular does not mean less acceptable.

> I lighted three candles.
> I lit three candles.

Both *lit* and *lighted* can also be adjectives, and again both are equally acceptable.

> He saw her across the lighted dance floor.
> He saw her across the lit dance floor.

LITERALLY: PLEASE TAKE THIS LITERALLY

The word *literally* means "in a literal sense." Exactly. Without exaggeration. Word for word. When you say your head is literally going to explode, there are a lot of people whose blood pressure literally rises as they imagine putting lit firecrackers in your ears to make your sentence correct. It's best to avoid using *literally* to add extra emphasis to your writing.

LOG IN VERSUS *LOG ON*: LOG ME IN, COACH; I'M READY TO PLAY

Log in, *log on*, *log out*, and *log off* are all considered phrasal verbs: two-word verbs. *Log in* and *log on* are interchangeable, as are *log out* and *log off*.

> Please log off at the end of class.

If you use these words as adjectives before a noun, use a hyphen.

I hate the flashing graphics on the <u>log-in</u> page.

MAY VERSUS *CAN*

(See *Can* Versus May.)

MAY VERSUS *MIGHT*: I WISH I MAY, I WISH I MIGHT

The difference between *may* and *might* is subtle. If something is likely to happen, use *may*.

> Squiggly <u>may</u> come over later.
> Aardvark <u>may</u> get dressed up.

If something is a mighty stretch, use *might*.

> Squiggly <u>might</u> win the lottery.
> Aardvark <u>might</u> grow wings and fly.

Might is also the past tense of *may*.

> Squiggly <u>might</u> have called Aardvark yesterday;
> we're not sure.

MORE THAN VERSUS *OVER*: MORE THAN YOU WANT TO KNOW

Is it OK to use *more than* and *over* interchangeably to mean "in excess of"? Intelligent, well-meaning people say no (as do some snotty, disagreeable people).

Technically, *over* is a preposition that usually means "above" or "on top of."

> We flew <u>over</u> Mount Saint Helens.

More than acts as an adjectival phrase.

> I'm sure he ate <u>more than</u> five cookies.

This is a pet peeve for some people, but it's not one for me. So I'm going to take a stand and say this "rule" is outdated and you can choose the one that sounds better in your sentence.

For example, you could say you ran *"over* a mile" or you ran *"more than* a mile." Either way, you'd be a bit tired.

You could also say the price is "not *over* five dollars" or "not *more than* five dollars."

On the other hand (yes, I know I'm waffling, but I also don't want to get you in trouble), there's no reason not to follow the sticklers' "rule," unless the "right" way sounds very strange.

One last thing—whichever way you go on this debate, remember that *than* is spelled *T-H-A-N*, not *T-H-E-N*. (See *Then* Versus *Than*.)

NAUSEOUS VERSUS *NAUSEATED*: THIS MAKES ME SICK

Many people say they are nauseous when their stomach is queasy. Using *nauseous* in that way sometimes makes sticklers nauseated because they stick with the rule that *nauseous* means to induce nausea, whereas *nauseated* means you feel sick.

> The <u>nauseous</u> fumes permeated the room.
> The fumes were <u>nauseating</u>.
> We all felt <u>nauseated</u>.

Although only the most irritating people will judge you on your grammar when you're describing how sick you feel, it's best to avoid *nauseous* altogether. Use *nauseated* when you're well enough to care about word choice and *nauseating* when you're describing something that makes you sick.

OF: LEAVE *OF* OFF

You may be shocked, but it's true that you don't need *of* to follow *off*. The *of* is unnecessary fluff.

> Get your feet <u>off of</u> the couch.

(You don't need to listen because it's incorrect.)

Get your feet <u>off</u> the couch.

(I would get those feet off—now!)

ON LINE VERSUS ONLINE: TROLLING THE INTERNET

When you're on the Internet, you're online and it's one word.

I learned Latin through an <u>online</u> class.

ONE VERSUS YOU

One and *you* are both pronouns you can use to refer to someone else. Or should I have said they are both pronouns one can use to refer to someone else? They mean the same thing; using *one* is just a more formal way of saying it. Occasionally, *one* is the better choice because it sounds less accusing than *you*.

<u>One</u> should always refrain from picking <u>one's</u> nose in public.

<u>You</u> should always refrain from picking <u>your</u> nose in public.

Nevertheless, although it's grammatically acceptable to use *one* as a gender-neutral singular pronoun, you'll probably want to stick with *you* most of the time.

OVER VERSUS MORE THAN

(See *More Than* Versus *Over*.)

Prepositions: English Is a Crazy Language

People who didn't grow up speaking English usually want to know why we use a particular preposition in a specific phrase.

Do people suffer *from a disease* or suffer *with a disease*? Are we *in a restaurant* or *at a restaurant*? Do you *run into* or *run across* someone?

I'm a native English speaker, so my first thought is usually something like "I don't know why; *run into* just sounds right," and sometimes either option seems correct.

Choosing between *by accident* and *on accident* turns out to be a matter of age. Most people over forty say *by accident*, and most people under thirty-five say *on accident*.

There's nothing grammatically incorrect about using *on line* to mean standing *in line* (such as standing in line at the movie theater); it just sounds strange to people who aren't used to hearing it. This is a regional idiosyncrasy—people clustered on the East Coast say *on line*. For people in the rest of the country, being *in line* is much more common.

Crazy, right? (For more on prepositions, see section 1-30.)

PRESUME VERSUS *ASSUME*
(See *Assume* Versus *Presume*.)

PRINCIPAL VERSUS *PRINCIPLE*: BE A PAL
Here's an old trick to remember how to spell the head of your school—your principal is your pal.

But *principal* is more than a noun. It's also an adjective meaning "most important."

> Squiggly's <u>principal</u> activity was practicing gymnastics.

Principle, on the other hand, is only a noun and means "a fundamental belief."

> Squiggly lived by the <u>principle</u> that food is good and more food is better.

> Squiggly lived by his principal <u>principle</u> that food is good and more food is better.

SEMIANNUAL VERSUS *BIANNUAL*: EATING SEMISWEET CHOCOLATE ON A BICYCLE

The prefixes *bi* and *semi* are different. *Semi* means half (you can remember it by thinking that semisweet chocolate is only half sweet), but *bi* means twice or two. That means *biweekly* can be used for every two weeks or twice every week. I can't believe nobody has solved this problem!

My advice is to avoid using *biweekly* and *bimonthly*. Instead, say "twice a week" or "every other week"—more people are likely to come to your meeting.

SIMPLE VERSUS *SIMPLISTIC*: IT'S SIMPLY MARVELOUS

You may not watch HGTV, but I do, and they often make a common error: they say *simplistic* when they mean *simple*. A simple design is clean and easy. A simplistic design is overly simplified. *Simple* is a good thing; *simplistic* is a bad thing.

> Her explanation confused me because it was <u>simplistic</u>.
> I love it when they make things <u>simple</u> for me.

SINCE VERSUS *BECAUSE*

(See *Because* Versus *Since*.)

SIT VERSUS *SET*: SIT, STAY, ROLL OVER

The story with *sit* and *set* is similar to the story with *lay* and *lie* (see that entry in this chapter): *set* requires a direct object, *sit* does not.

Fortunately, I have a Quick and Dirty Tip to help you remember the difference between the two words: when you're training a dog, you tell her to sit. My first dog's name was Dude, so we would tell her, "Sit, Dude. Sit."

That is how you use *sit*—for the action of sitting.

Dude, <u>sit</u>!

I wish Dude would <u>sit</u> on her bed instead of on mine.

Set, on the other hand, requires an object. I would set Dude's leash on the table, but she would still think we were going for a walk.

If I <u>set</u> her leash on the table, maybe she'll forget about going for a walk.

She saw me <u>set</u> it down, but she still thinks we're going.

A dog (or person) sits, and you set things, like leashes, down.

STATIONARY VERSUS *STATIONERY*: STAY ABSOLUTELY STILL

Stationery is paper.

My grandmother sent me a box of <u>stationery</u> so I would be sure to send her thank-you notes.

Stationary means not moving. Still.

> No matter how hard he pedaled on the <u>stationary</u> bike, Squiggly never left the room.

A Quick and Dirty Tip to help you remember? When I think of stationery (writing paper), I think of how everyone sends e-mail messages now (or text messages) rather than writing notes on actual paper. The *e* in *e-mail* helps me think of writing, and stationery is writing paper. You can also remember that when you are stationary, you are often standing. Since *standing* has an *a*, it reminds me to put that second *a* in *stationary.*

SUPPOSABLY VERSUS *SUPPOSEDLY*: WHAT'S YOUR SUPPOSED EXCUSE?

I wish I could tell you that **supposably** isn't a word, but it is. The problem is that it doesn't mean the same thing as **supposedly**, and most people who use it are doing so incorrectly.

The word you usually want is **supposedly**, which means roughly "assumed to be true" and almost always includes a hint of sarcasm or disbelief.

> <u>Supposedly</u>, he canceled our date because of a family emergency.

> She <u>supposedly</u> did her homework, but she said the dog ate it.

Supposably means "it is supposable," "it is conceivable," or "arguably." It is a word valid only in American English; the British wisely refuse to accept it.

THAN VERSUS *THEN*
(See *Then* Versus *Than*.)

THAT VERSUS *WHICH*: "WHICH'S" BREW

You can show off your knowledge of restrictive and nonrestrictive clauses here, as well as flaunt your ability to use a comma wisely.

Deciding when to use *that* or *which* can overwhelm people.

To make things as simple as possible, use *that* before a restrictive clause and *which* before everything else.

A **restrictive element** is just part of a sentence you can't get rid of because it specifically restricts the noun. Remember Grammar Girl's love of chocolate in section 2-19?

Desserts <u>that</u> contain chocolate please Grammar Girl.

The words *that contain chocolate* restrict the kind of desserts you're talking about. Without them, the meaning of the sentence would change. Without them, you would be saying that all desserts please Grammar Girl, not just the ones with chocolate. (Note also that you don't need commas around the words *that contain chocolate*.)

Do all cars use hybrid technology? Is every leaf green? The answer is no. Only some cars have hybrid technology, and only some leaves are green. It would change the meaning to throw out the restrictive element in the examples below, so you need a *that*. Notice the lack of commas around the restrictive element.

Cars <u>that have hybrid technology</u> get great gas mileage.
Leaves <u>that are green</u> contain chlorophyll.

Because a **nonrestrictive element** is something that can be left off without changing the meaning of the sentence, use *which*. A nonrestrictive element is simply additional information.

Chocolate desserts, <u>which are her favorites</u>, please Grammar Girl.

Leaving out the words *which are her favorites* doesn't change the meaning of the sentence. Nonrestrictive phrases are surrounded by commas.

A Quick and Dirty Tip? If you think of the Wicked Witch (*Which*) of the West from *The Wizard of Oz*, you know it's OK to throw her out. You won't change the meaning of the sentence, so you can throw out the *which* (or witch) phrase, commas and all.

Remember how at the beginning of this section I said, "To make things as simple as possible, use *that* before a restrictive clause and *which* before everything else?" That is the simplified rule, and if you do it that way, you'll always get it right; but in practice, you can also sometimes use *which* before restrictive clauses. Stick with the simple rule and don't sweat it, but when you see someone use *which* before a restrictive clause, don't automatically assume it's wrong.

THAT VERSUS *WHO*: WHO SAYS GRAMMAR IS EASY?

The Quick and Dirty Tip is to use *that* when you are talking about an object and *who* when you are talking about a person. That's the safe way to go.

What do you do when you are talking about something animate but not human? It can go either way. I would never refer to my dog as anything less than a *who*, but my fish could probably be a *that*.

Except That . . .

You can use *whose*, which is the possessive form of *who*, to refer to both people and things because English doesn't have a possessive form of *that*. So it's fine to say "the desk *whose* top is cluttered with grammar books," even though it is obviously ridiculous to say "the desk who is made of cherry wood."

Personally, I would rewrite: "The top of the desk is cluttered with grammar books."

THEN VERSUS *THAN*: AND THEN THERE WERE NONE

Do you confuse *then* and *than*? Don't worry; you're not alone. Lots of people get confused, but you have Grammar Girl to come to your rescue.

Then has an element of time. For example, it can mean "next" or "at that time."

> We ate and <u>then</u> we went to the movies.
> Movies were a lot cheaper back <u>then</u>.

Than conveys a comparison.

> DVDs are more expensive <u>than</u> videocassettes.
> Aardvark is taller <u>than</u> Squiggly.

The Quick and Dirty Tip is that *th<u>a</u>n* and *comp<u>a</u>rison* both have the letter *a* in them, and *th<u>e</u>n* and *tim<u>e</u>* both have the letter *e*.

THERE VERSUS *THEIR* VERSUS *THEY'RE*: THERE YOU GO

The word *there* might fill up a book of its own—it can be a pronoun, an adverb, a noun, and an adjective.

> <u>There</u> are too many choices, yet none of them are right. (pronoun)

> Squiggly's shoes were <u>there</u> all the time. (adverb)

> He walked from here to <u>there</u>. (noun)

> That girl <u>there</u> won the spelling bee. (adjective)

Their is a possessive pronoun.

> <u>Their</u> shoes match their hats.

They're is a contraction of *they are*.

> <u>They're</u> planning on owning shoes that match all their hats.

TILL VERSUS *UNTIL*: UNTIL WE MEET AGAIN

When you're talking about a period of time that must elapse before something happens, *till* and *until* are equivalent. Don't believe it? Check a dictionary. *Till* actually came first, and *until* followed more recently.

'Til (with an apostrophe) is also an acceptable shortened form of *until*, but the *American Heritage Dictionary of the English Language, fourth edition*, says the form is "etymologically incorrect." It's best to avoid *'til*.

TO VERSUS *TOO* VERSUS *TWO*: IT'S ALL TOO MUCH

To is a preposition.

> Take me <u>to</u> your leader.

Too means "also" or "as well" or "excessively."

> I couldn't possibly eat the banana cream pie <u>too</u> (also).
> This chocolate cream pie is <u>too</u> (excessively) rich for me.

Two is a number. It comes after one and before three.

> Aardvark and Squiggly are <u>two</u> of Grammar Girl's friends.

Two Words . . . or One?

The English language has a bunch of words that have different meanings (and spellings sometimes) when they are one or two words. We're only going to deal with some of them.

Anymore (now or at present) versus *any more* (something additional or further).

> Grammar Girl doesn't wear her hair short <u>anymore</u>.

> Do you have <u>any more</u> to say about Grammar Girl's hair?

Already (deals with time in the past) versus *all ready* (everyone or everything is geared up and prepared).

Is everybody here <u>already</u>?
Is everybody here <u>all ready</u>?

Altogether (completely) versus *all together* (a group).

He is <u>altogether</u> dressed, from his hat to his shoes.

We watched the debates <u>all together</u> at Squiggly's house.

Often, the *all* in *all together* is redundant and can be left out without changing the meaning of the sentence.

Everyday (common) versus *every day* (each day).

Except for Saturday and Sunday, going to school is an <u>everyday</u> occurrence.

I eat dinner <u>every day</u>.

Something (a pronoun) versus *some thing* (an adjective and a noun).

I know <u>something</u> about Aardvark, but I'm not telling.
He had <u>some things</u> hanging in his locker.

USE TO VERSUS *USED TO*: I USED TO KNOW THE DIFFERENCE

The right way is *used to* with a *d* on the end. People get confused about this phrase because the *d* and *t* sounds between the words are easy to run together, but it's easy to remember that *used to* is the right form, not *use to*.

The Quick and Dirty Tip is that when you say you used to do

something, you are talking about the past, and you make most verbs past tense by adding *d* or *ed* to the end.

Just as you say you heav<u>ed</u> yourself into the kayak or twirl<u>ed</u> in a circle, you say you us<u>ed</u> to have a lot more fun.

WELL VERSUS GOOD
(See *Good* Versus *Well*.)

WHETHER VERSUS IF
(See *If* Versus *Whether*.)

WHICH VERSUS THAT
(See *That* Versus *Which*.)

WHICH VERSUS WHO: HORTON HEARS A WHO
Very simple. *Which* is for things; *who* is for people.

> <u>Who</u> is the person you'll listen to when deciding <u>which</u> word is correct?

WHO VERSUS THAT
(See *That* Versus *Who*.)

WHO VERSUS WHOM: WHOM DO YOU LOVE?
You've always wondered how to use *who* and *whom*. I know you have! Maybe you don't sit on a grassy hill under an oak tree fondly wondering, but when you have to write a sentence that may need a *whom*, suddenly you want to know.

The words *who* and *whom* are both pronouns (see section 1-12). You know the difference between subject and object, but I'll repeat it here.

Subject—the doer of the action; the one who acts.

Object—the receiver of the action; the one who lets it all happen to her or him.

Use *who* when you are referring to the subject of a clause and *whom* when you are referring to the object of a clause.

Whom does Grammar Girl love?

Use *whom* because you are asking about the object—the target of Grammar Girl's love.

When is it OK to use *who*? If you wanted to know what person loves Grammar Girl (I am receiving the love and am the object in this sentence), then you would use *who*.

Who loves Grammar Girl?

You are asking about the subject—the one taking action (the one who is loving)—so you use *who*.

The Quick and Dirty Tip is to ask yourself if you could hypothetically answer the question with the word *him*. If you can, you use *whom*, and *him* and *whom* both end with the letter *m*.

[Who or Whom] should we invite to the party?
We should invite him to the party. (The correct choice is *whom*.)

[Who or Whom] is coming to the party?
He is coming to the party. (The correct choice is *who*.)

WHOEVER VERSUS WHOMEVER: WHATEVER!

As with *who* and *whom*, the choice between their derivatives, *whoever* and *whomever*, depends on identifying the subject and object position. This time, however, you have to identify the position in two implied clauses that have been joined by *whoever* or *whomever*. You can use the same "him" test we used for *who* and *whom*, but now you need both implied pronouns to be in the object case to use *whomever*. If you don't have two *hims*—in other words, two object pronouns—use *whoever*.

> Give the doughnuts to <u>him</u>. <u>He</u> arrived first.
> (one object pronoun and one subject pronoun)
> Give the doughnuts to <u>whoever</u> arrived first.
>
> I'll give the doughnuts to <u>him</u>. You choose <u>him</u>.
> (two object pronouns)
> I'll give the doughnuts to <u>whomever</u> you choose.

Chapter Five

Your Right to Write

ARE YOU READY for the big secret?

Writing is hard.

Sure, it's not as physically hard as digging a hole in granite with a plastic fork (you know, the kind that breaks when you try to eat spaghetti), but I bet your brain thinks it's doing hard labor when trying to write.

Do you have hesitation or even fear when you see a blank screen or page? I admit that I do sometimes. Some days writing seems downright painful.

Yet even when I think writing is close to impossible, suddenly a moment comes (after a lot of hard work) when my thoughts connect, my words pour out, and my writing has a rhythm that adds to the meaning and even the beauty of my piece.

Why am I telling you this? So that when you get that loud "Oh no, I can't write" voice whirling in your head, you don't feel alone. Writers—professional writers—get writer's block at different points in their lives. Some writers get it monthly, weekly, or even daily.

To stop that screaming voice, remember that you have all the tools for writing and that I'm here to help. I can tell you where to look for the usual problems in writing, what to watch out for, why you must proofread your work, when to start a new paragraph, and how to rewrite.

As you write, you'll develop your own style. All writers do. Everyone's writing voice is as distinctive as their speaking voice. (Yes, *everyone* is a singular noun, and I'm using *their* as a gender-neutral singular pronoun. I'm so wild.) You may be able to impersonate Stephenie Meyer or Rick Riordan, but why be a clone? Discover your own voice.

I can't teach you style. You have to find that for yourself through work and over time, but I can give you tools to help you along the way.

Follow me, grasshopper.

Brilliant Words of Wisdom

Ignore everything in this chapter until you finish your first draft.

When you write your first draft—whether it's a term paper or a creative writing piece—just write. Don't think about rules, suggestions, spelling, or commas.

If it's a term paper and you've done your research, if you have your facts and have figured out the organization ahead of time (or even if you're still feeling your way through), just write.

If you're doing creative writing, just write.

Don't judge yourself or your writing when you first start a project. If you're yelling at yourself for some stupid word choice, you'll never move on. The blank screen will loom larger.

Instead of listening to the yelling voice in your head, think

---

of me sitting beside you, whispering that your word choice is perfect and that you should keep going, that writing is hard and you're doing great. Keep writing.

There's plenty of time and opportunity to edit and re-write, and that's what you should do: edit, rewrite, edit, rewrite, edit, rewrite, edit, rewrite, etc. If you turn in your first draft, you haven't done even close to your best. This book went through at least six rounds of edits, and I know fiction writers who have done as many as twenty rounds of edits on their novels.

WORDINESS

Wordiness bugs people. If you don't believe me, I would be happy to show you the gazillion e-mail messages I get complaining about it. These notes are often laced with serious venom. It's as if the complainer has been locked in a box and forced to listen to the same wordy phrase over and over, again and again.

I'm so embarrassed. The phrases *over and over* and *again and again* are a form of wordiness.

Wordiness creeps into your writing, and it appears in many forms, such as unnecessary words; repeating phrases, words, or thoughts; and overwriting.

Never fear—we'll handle them one by one.

Unnecessary Words

Some writers write perfectly correct sentences but use more words than are necessary.

> If you want to, go ahead and wear a Hawaiian shirt, but leave the first button not buttoned up.

The phrase *go ahead and* is unnecessary. Wordiness mistakes like that are easy to make in writing because we use them in speech.

> If you want to, wear a Hawaiian shirt, but leave the first button not buttoned up.

The word *up* doesn't add information. It doesn't do anything, and it sounds awkward.

> If you want to, wear a Hawaiian shirt, but leave the first button not buttoned.

Notice that the word *button* is repeated. To fix that, you need to do more than delete some words; you'll need to change a couple of words so that the sentence makes sense.

> If you want to, wear a Hawaiian shirt, but leave the first button undone.

You could tighten it even more.

> If you wear a Hawaiian shirt, leave the top unbuttoned.

Here's another sentence that, with tweaking, could be written more concisely:

> Squiggly thought that he might be able to figure out what he might buy Grammar Girl for her upcoming birthday.

The *might be able to* and *upcoming* are not serving any purpose. What other birthday would it be but the upcoming one? (If it were a birthday two years in the future, the writer would specifically say that.)

> Squiggly thought that he could figure out what he would buy Grammar Girl for her birthday.

That sentence highlights Squiggly's uncertainty, but if that wasn't the main point, the sentence could be rewritten to be even trimmer.

> Squiggly knew what he would buy Grammar Girl
> for her birthday.

Here's another sentence with lots of unnecessary phrases:

> Grammar Girl's reason for why she cleaned up the whole
> house was sort of because she thought that her guests,
> when they came in, might trip over her belongings left on
> the floor when they walked around her house.

Let's get rid of the nonessential phrases.

> Grammar Girl's reason for why she cleaned up the whole
> house was sort of because she thought that her guests,
> when they came in, might trip over her belongings left on
> the floor when they walked around her house.

> Grammar Girl cleaned the house because she thought
> her guests might trip over her belongings left on the floor
> when they walked around. (Much better. It's almost
> finished, but we'll do a little more on it later.)

On the other hand, sometimes wordiness can serve a purpose.
I wanted to tell you that I'm not coming to your party sounds less cold
than *I'm not coming to your party.*

The difference is that *I wanted to tell you that* (or *I thought you
should know that*) serves a purpose (easing into bad news), while
the other phrases or unnecessary words we've reviewed didn't.

Excessive Prepositions

People sometimes use prepositions unnecessarily, or they use two
prepositions when one would suffice.

> Please don't sit <u>down</u> on the freshly painted chair. (How
> else does one sit but down?)

Please don't sit on the freshly painted chair. (better)

Raise your hand up when you need to leave the room.
(Your hand automatically goes up when you raise it.)

Raise your hand when you need to leave the room.
(better)

Up until Grammar Girl met Squiggly, she didn't know that
she loved snails. (*Until* doesn't need any help from *up*,
which is an extra preposition.)

Until Grammar Girl met Squiggly, she didn't know that she
loved snails. (better)

Nixing the Horrid *Of*

Almost everyone has bad writing habits. One of mine is that I overuse the word *of*. I'm not the only one; overusing *of* is a common
writing problem, so it deserves its own section.

Of is a preposition, and although it's not an inherently evil word,
overusing it can make your writing sound passive and fussy. Here's
an example of a bad sentence:

She is the sister of Aardvark. (ick)

It makes me cringe just to see it.

She is Aardvark's sister. (better)

See? You don't need the *of*. The sentence sounds more straightforward without it.

Only use the *of* in that horrid way to avoid a double possessive.

She is Aardvark's neighbor's sister. (hard to follow)

She is the sister <u>of</u> Aardvark's neighbor. (acceptable to avoid a double possessive; see section 3-35)

Useless *of*s can slip into your writing without being noticed if you aren't careful. I often go back through my documents looking for *of*s to delete.

Get off <u>of</u> me.
Get off me. (better)

You might write the following:

Squiggly put all <u>of</u> his ducks in a row. (OK)

The sentence is fine, but you could tighten it.

Squiggly put all his ducks in a row. (better)
Squiggly put his ducks in a row. (better)

The *of* is not needed.
On the other hand, there are good ways to use the word *of*.

Please bring me a bucket <u>of</u> water.

You have to write it that way to show you want a bucket with water in it. Without the *of*, the sentence means something different.

Please bring me a water bucket.

In that sentence the reader could think you are asking for a bucket that is meant to hold only water.

An exception, another idiom, is that the word *couple* is usually followed by *of*, as in

A <u>couple of</u> chickens crossed the road.

Nevertheless, it's a good idea to search out your *of*s and make sure they are necessary.

You Can Say That Again! On Second Thought—Don't!

If you get irritated by repeatedly hearing your parents' stories, you can understand how redundancy can annoy other people. Rather than focusing on the positive message, one of my podcast listeners angrily noticed the redundancy of this sign: SEASON'S GREETINGS AND HAPPY HOLIDAYS.

I bet people will never tell him that they love *and* adore him!

Redundancy is a subspecies of wordiness—not only are the words unnecessary, but you've already made the same point. Sometimes people repeat the specific word or use more than one phrase that says the same thing.

Can you catch the redundancies in this sentence?

> Right now, Aardvark wanted to make sure that at this point in time Grammar Girl was going to heartily and utterly celebrate her birthday now.

A sentence can have repetitive phrases even if the words aren't right next to each other.

Right now and *now* have the same meaning. In fact, you don't need the *right* in front of *now* because now is now! You can't be any "now-er" than *now*.

> Aardvark wanted to make sure that at this point in time Grammar Girl was going to heartily and utterly celebrate her birthday now.

At this point in time also means *now*. (Tricky, huh? Three ways of writing *now*!)

> Aardvark wanted to make sure that Grammar Girl was going to heartily and utterly celebrate her birthday now.

Heartily and utterly is redundant.

Aardvark wanted to make sure that Grammar Girl was going to heartily celebrate her birthday now. (ta-da!)

The reason...is because is a redundant phrase that sends people off the deep end because to say *the reason* implies *because*. Consider this sentence and the two simplified versions that follow:

The reason you love grammar is because you love rules. (redundant)

The reason you love grammar is that you love rules. (acceptable)

You love grammar because you love rules. (better)

Remember the sentence that had lots of unnecessary phrases? Here it is again:

Grammar Girl's reason for why she cleaned up the whole house was sort of because she thought that her guests, when they came in, might trip over her belongings left on the floor when they walked around her house.

We cut it down to

Grammar Girl cleaned the house because she thought her guests might trip over her belongings left on the floor when they walked around.

But now that we're dealing with discarding repetitive phrases, I would cut the sentence even more.

Grammar Girl cleaned the house because she thought her guests might trip over her belongings ~~left on the floor when they walked around~~.

> Grammar Girl cleaned the house because she thought
> her guests might trip over her belongings.

I think *trip over* covers *when they walked around,* although the meanings aren't identical. People only trip when walking or running. Also, people would only trip over things on the floor, so that part is redundant too.

SOME COMMON REDUNDANT PHRASES			
YUCK	**BETTER**	**YUCK**	**BETTER**
100% complete	complete	natural instinct	instinct
back behind	behind	new innovation	innovation
brief moment	moment	pair of twins	twins
completely filled	filled	past history	history
complete stranger	stranger	personal friend	friend
connect together	connect	point in time	time
down below	down *or* below	postpone until later	postpone
each and every	each *or* every	price point	price
end result	result	regular routine	routine
exact same	exact *or* same	serious danger	danger
first of all	first	start out	start
frozen ice	ice	sudden impulse	impulse
grow in size	grow	total destruction	destruction
introduced a new	introduced	true fact	fact
join together	join	two equal halves	two halves
little baby	baby	two polar opposites	opposites
live witness	witness	visible to the eye	visible
might possibly	might		

Again with the Redundancy

People often write redundantly when they are using acronyms and initialisms because they forget what the letters represent. For example, *PIN number* is redundant because the *N* in *PIN* stands for *number*, so people are writing *personal identification number number*. *HIV virus* is redundant because *V* stands for *virus*. *ATM machine* isn't correct because *M* stands for *machine*.

When you use an acronym, think about the words it stands for so that you don't add a redundant word at the end. If you are afraid people won't know what you mean if you use the acronym without the redundant word, then don't use the acronym—write out the whole thing.

Using foreign words can also tempt people into redundancy to make their meaning clear. Take the phrase *chai tea*. It's redundant because *chai* is the Hindi word for "tea."

Marketers could create campaigns that explain the foreign word's meaning—try our chai: a delicious tea made with milk, sugar, and spices—but space is often limited in stores and on signs, so it's not surprising that the concept gets shortened to *chai tea*. As a result, in America, the phrase *chai tea* comes to mean a particular kind of tea made in the Indian style. If you wish to avoid redundancy, just ask for chai.

One More Time with Feeling

Can you see what's wrong with the paragraph below? I'll admit I've exaggerated the problem.

> Aardvark angered Squiggly so much, and Squiggly was upset, so he wouldn't talk with him, but Aardvark didn't know how to apologize. Hurt by Aardvark, Squiggly didn't want to talk with him, and Aardvark didn't know what to

do. Because Squiggly was upset with Aardvark, he wouldn't answer his phone calls.

You're right—each sentence says the same thing, only slightly differently (try to ignore the confusing pronouns, extra words, and awkwardness in each sentence). In the above paragraph, I didn't know how to say exactly what I meant in one sentence, so I wrote three sentences that meant practically the same thing but covered slightly different ideas.

If you left the paragraph like this and handed in your paper, this paragraph would deserve to be called wordy. If you gave yourself time to edit, you could trim that paragraph to one sentence.

> Squiggly was too angry to talk to Aardvark, and except for phoning, Aardvark didn't know how to apologize.

Or you might decide that two sentences are better, but the sentences wouldn't have identical information.

> Although Aardvark tried phoning, Squiggly was too angry to talk to him. Aardvark didn't know how to apologize.

Or you might keep the three sentences but let the logic progress from one sentence to the next.

> Squiggly was too angry to talk to Aardvark. Aardvark wanted to apologize and tried phoning. Squiggly wouldn't answer.

They aren't brilliant, but the sentences are clearer and not repetitive.

You So Very Much Don't Want to Overuse *So* and *Very*

One of my podcast listeners asked me if the sentence below is acceptable:

She is sooooo very happy that she is going to the prom.

The words *so* and *very* are often used as intensifiers, meaning they allow you to express that you are happier than just happy.

In formal writing, both words are looked down on, but *so* (by itself) is considered worse than *very.*

When you're speaking, emphasizing the word *so* seems to add punch to a simple statement—"I'm sooooo happy"—which is fine in informal conversation but should be avoided in writing (even without the extra *o*'s).

On the other hand, when *so* is paired with *that*, it becomes more acceptable in writing.

> Squiggly was <u>so</u> happy. (wrong)
> Squiggly was <u>so</u> happy <u>that</u> he jumped for joy. (right)

When you say "Squiggly was so happy that he jumped for joy," *so* becomes an adverb related to the degree of happiness instead of a vague intensifier. In other words, *so* leads into a thought about *how* happy Squiggly was. How happy was he? So happy that he jumped for joy.

Unlike with the word *so*, it's not considered a mistake to use the word *very* by itself for emphasis. Nevertheless, don't overdo it.

Instead of *I was very hungry*, it's better to search for a more creative adjective and write *I was famished* or *I was ravenous*. Replacing two simple words (*very hungry*) with one descriptive word (*ravenous*) makes your writing tighter and usually more interesting.

You don't have to banish *very* from the language. E. B. White, coauthor of the famous guide *The Elements of Style*, used the repetition of *very* in a letter, writing, "It was a day of very white clouds, very blue skies, and very dark green spruces." The repeated *very*s create a strong rhythm. The effect would be lost if White had written, "It was a day of snowy clouds, oceanic skies, and evergreen spruces."

Finally, don't get *very* confused with *vary*, which is a verb that means "to differ or change."

That Problem

Some people also get all riled up about the word *that*. They shout that it's redundant! Unnecessary! An abomination!

Well, I agree (I wouldn't go as far as abomination), but only sometimes.

When is it OK to omit the word *that* in a sentence?

The sentences *The turkey sandwich I ate yesterday had too much mayonnaise* and *The turkey sandwich that I ate yesterday had too much mayonnaise* mean the same thing. In this case it's perfectly fine to delete *that*.

If your sentence already has another *that* or two, you don't want to complicate it more by adding yet another *that*.

> I understand <u>that</u> she would prefer <u>that</u> people not call her Miss Grammar Girl.

The two *that*s don't add clarity to the sentence. I would rewrite it (and please don't call me Miss Grammar Girl!).

> I understand she would prefer <u>that</u> people not call her Miss Grammar Girl.

Sometimes a sentence doesn't even need one *that*.

> Aardvark told her <u>that</u> she was the one <u>that</u> he wanted to go with. (two unnecessary *that*s)

> Aardvark told her she was the one he wanted to go with. (better without the *that*s)

So when is *that* necessary?

Unfortunately, many people take their *that* phobia to extremes and delete *that*s even when they are needed for clarity. Here's an example of a sentence that confuses readers when you omit the word *that*:

Aardvark maintains Squiggly's yard is too large.

Because *that* is missing, the reader could initially believe that Aardvark takes care of (maintains) Squiggly's lawn. The meaning isn't clear until they reach the phrase *is too large*.

Aardvark maintains <u>that</u> Squiggly's yard is too large.

This sentence is clearer with *that* included—no reader would ever think Aardvark is mowing the lawn. The *that* signals readers at the beginning that Aardvark just has an opinion.

Use *that* if there is any chance a reader can become confused without it. Your reader shouldn't need to reread your sentence to understand it.

A Final Word on *That*

When you're deciding whether to keep or omit your *that*, consider how your sentence flows. Many times, it's a matter of personal preference. Some people think adding *that* improves the flow of the sentence and makes it easier for the reader to understand. Others believe they should delete every seemingly unnecessary *that* because they want to be brief. I'm all for cutting unnecessary words, but I like to keep my *that* if it helps the rhythm of the sentence. You'll have to judge whether using *that* in your particular sentence improves or hurts its flow. Sometimes it helps to read your paragraph aloud to see if you've got the right rhythm. Also, it is helpful to know your teachers' stances on "unnecessary" *that*s.

There Are and *There Is:* Extra Fluff

Starting sentences with *There are* and *There is* is grammatically correct, but the words are often unnecessary fluff.

> There are many people who hate rain. (OK)
> Many people hate rain. (better)

Not only are the words unnecessary, but they can make your sentences sound weak and boring. Usually your sentence will be better with a stronger subject and verb.

Which of the following sounds more exciting and helps you get a better visual image? (Hint: It's the one marked "better.")

> There is a fly in my soup. (OK)
>
> A fly is swimming laps in my soup. (better)

In the above examples, *people* and *fly* are the true subjects of the sentences, so why hide them?

When your sentences start with *There are* or *There is*, try to rewrite them. If no amount of rewriting helps—if the rewrite is more awkward than the original sentence—it's OK to keep an occasional *There are* or *There is* in your papers.

Of course, you know to make sure that your verbs agree with your subjects. Don't write

> There is cheerleaders in the field. (nope)
> There are cheerleaders in the field. (yup)
> There is a cheerleader in the field. (yup)

ACTIVE VOICE VERSUS PASSIVE VOICE

Many people believe they should avoid the passive voice, but fewer people can define it.

I'll start with active voice because it's simpler. In an active sentence, the subject is doing the action. The following is a straightforward example:

Squiggly loves Grammar Girl.

Squiggly is the subject, and he is doing the action: he loves *Grammar Girl*, the object. (See sections 2-1 and 2-3 for an overview of subject versus object.)

In passive voice, the target of the action gets promoted to the subject position. Instead of writing *Squiggly loves Grammar Girl*, I would write

Grammar Girl is loved by Squiggly.

The subject of the sentence becomes *Grammar Girl*, but she isn't doing anything. Rather, she is the recipient of Squiggly's love. The focus of the sentence has changed from Squiggly to Grammar Girl.

A lot of people think all sentences that contain a form of the verb **to be** are in passive voice, but that isn't true. For example, the sentence *I am holding a pen* is in active voice although it uses the verb *am*, which is a form of **to be**. The passive form of that sentence is **The pen is being held by me**.

Active-voice sentences are stronger, usually shorter, and more direct than passive-voice sentences.

Passive sentences aren't incorrect, but often they aren't the best way to phrase your thoughts. Sometimes passive voice is awkward, and other times it's vague. Also, passive voice is wordy. You can tighten your writing if you use active voice more often than passive voice.

When you put sentences in passive voice, it's easy to omit the person who is responsible for the action. For example, *Aardvark is loved* is passive. The problem is that you don't know who loves Aardvark.

In fact, politicians often use passive voice intentionally to hide their own responsibility or hide who did the action. Pay attention to the news and listen to examples of passive voice: *Bombs were dropped* and *Shots were fired*.

On the other hand, sometimes passive voice is the best choice. If you truly don't know who is taking the action, then you can't name that person.

> The factory was torched.

More important, passive voice is useful, depending on the idea you want to highlight. If you were writing a mystery novel and you wanted to highlight the cookies because they are central to the story, passive voice is the best option.

> The cookies were stolen. (passive voice)
> Somebody stole the cookies. (active voice)

The difference is subtle, but in *The cookies were stolen*, the focus is on the cookies. In *Somebody stole the cookies*, the focus is on the unknown somebody.

> She was ignored by her friends. (passive voice)
> Her friends ignored her. (active voice)

Again, the difference is subtle, but in the first sentence, *she* is the focus.

Passive voice is helpful if you are writing a report and must maintain an impersonal and scientific position.

> Older people were found to have worse peripheral vision than younger people.

KEEP PARALLEL CONSTRUCTION

It's important to keep the structure within your sentences parallel. It can be as simple as being consistent with prepositions and articles or as intricate as making sure the same verb form is used.

> Grammar Girl rode on the Ferris wheel, carousel, and the roller coaster. (wrong)

To make the sentence consistent, you have three choices. Make sure *the* is in front of all the rides, put *the* before only the first ride, or put *on the* before each ride.

> Grammar Girl rode on <u>the</u> Ferris wheel, <u>the</u> carousel, and <u>the</u> roller coaster.

> Grammar Girl rode on the Ferris wheel, carousel, and roller coaster.

> Grammar Girl rode <u>on the</u> Ferris wheel, <u>on the</u> carousel, and <u>on the</u> roller coaster.

When I read the sentences aloud (please join in!), I think the first one sounds best, so I would choose that.

Can you figure out what's wrong with the sentence below?

> Grammar Girl reads the dictionary and ate ice cream.

As much as I love doing both things, in that sentence I seem to be reading the dictionary now, but I ate ice cream in the past. The verb tenses must agree, or the sentence isn't parallel. I'll make them both past tense.

> Grammar Girl <u>read</u> the dictionary and <u>ate</u> ice cream.

Can you figure out why the next sentence doesn't work?

> Grammar Girl reads the dictionary and eating ice cream.

The verb forms aren't parallel. Either Grammar Girl is reading and eating or she reads and eats. From purely a "how it sounds" point of view, I would choose

> Grammar Girl is <u>reading</u> the dictionary and <u>eating</u> ice cream.

AWKWARDNESS

Sometimes things aren't technically wrong or wordy; they're just painfully awkward.

Awkwardness can stem from a sentence that sounds ungraceful. It may be because the rhythm isn't right or because of a wrong word choice, which sometimes happens if you plug in a random synonym from the thesaurus, rather than the one that is accurate.

Poor sentence structure also causes awkwardness.

Imagine you're writing a lovely sentence, and then you run smack into a double *the*. Oh, the horror!

> Have you heard the *The Fast and the Furious* soundtrack?

It's technically correct to write *the* twice because the second *the* is part of the title, but whether it's right or wrong, if you turn that in to an English teacher, it will be circled with a red pen and marked AWK for awkward. Rewrite the sentence to avoid the problem.

> Have you heard the soundtrack for *The Fast and the Furious*?

METAPHORS AND SIMILES: WRITING IS LIKE SKATING ON A POND

Metaphors and similes highlight how two different ideas or things are similar. They use the qualities of one thing to help the reader understand a different idea or point of view in a new way or with deeper insight.

The difference between metaphors and similes is that similes hit you over the head with the comparison by using an explicit word such as *like* or *as*. When Jon Bon Jovi sings "My heart is like an open highway," that's a simile because he uses the word *like* to directly compare his heart to an open highway.

Christina Aguilera sings "Since you've arrived like an angel from the sky," in her song "Without You." With those few words, you know how she feels about the guy and how wonderful he is. That's also a simile because it uses the word *like*.

Metaphors, on the other hand, don't use direct comparison words. Tom Cochrane's "Life Is a Highway" is a metaphor because there's no word such as *like* or *as*. Metaphors can be more subtle.

Duffy's "Stepping Stone" contains the lyric "But I will never be your stepping stone." This is a subtle metaphor. She's comparing herself to a stepping stone, singing that she won't be taken advantage of or used.

QUICK AND DIRTY TIP

You can remember the difference between similes and metaphors by remembering that *simile* has the letter *I* in it, just like the word *like*, which you often use in a simile.

You can also use metaphors and similes to help explain concepts that may confuse your readers. First, identify the point you want to explain. Then find a topic your readers might know well, and use a comparison to connect your point to the familiar topic to help your audience understand.

Imagine you're trying to explain podcasts to your grandmother and she doesn't get it. You might say, "A podcast is like a radio show that gets delivered to your computer or iPod, instead of over the radio."

Your grandmother understands that radio shows are audio shows that broadcast regularly. The simile equating a podcast to a radio show will help her use her existing knowledge to understand podcasts. It is a simile because you say "Podcasts are *like* radio shows," using the L-word (*like*) in the sentence, so we use the L-word (*simile*) to describe the comparison.

Next time you have a difficult idea to explain, try using a simile or a metaphor. It may take extra time to come up with the comparison, but once you have it, you can often get your point across faster and also help your audience remember what you said.

> ### Don't Mix or Overuse Your Metaphors and Similes
> The purpose of a metaphor is to enliven your writing and make your points clear. Too many metaphors and similes in the pot will spoil the stew. Remember, clarity is important.
>
> Don't compare an object or an idea to too many things at once, either—that will defeat your purpose and the reader won't understand what you're saying.
>
> Life is like a rubber band—it stretches to contain all that you can gather but breaks when you overload it like an electrical socket that can't take too many plugs.
>
> That confused sentence mixes two unrelated ideas: life is like a rubber band but also like an electrical socket.

AVOIDANCE: PROBLEMS IN WRITING

I know people say avoiding things is not a good policy. If you are afraid of spiders, some people suggest you learn about spiders or make a spider your pet.

I believe there are definitely things to avoid in grammar.

I would also avoid spiders!

Avoid Clichés Like the Plague

Clichés are like metaphors and similes gone bad.

Phrases are like furniture. For a short time they are comfortable and fashionable, but after a while they can become tired and over-used. That's what a cliché is: a tired, overused phrase. You've heard them a billion times—that's how they become clichés. Check these out:

A cliché is as plain as the nose on your face. If you could see eye to eye with your teachers, you'd realize that they'll get all bent out of shape unless you use the tried-and-true method of creating your own expressions. Take the bull by the horns, turn over a new leaf, and avoid clichés like the plague!

Clichés are OK every once in a while, but the very definition of *cliché* argues against their use: "a trite, overused expression."

SOME CLICHÉS, METAPHORS, AND SIMILES TO AVOID	
believe it or not	like a bump on a log
bored to tears	like the plague
don't count your chickens	old as the hills
before they hatch	on cloud nine
easy as pie	raining cats and dogs
get your ducks in a row	running a tight ship
greatest thing since	slept like a baby
sliced bread	thin as a rail
hard as nails	with a ten-foot pole
last but not least	

Overreliance on clichés can be a sign of weak writing because it usually means you couldn't think of a creative way to get your point across. Instead, you lazily borrowed a phrase someone else created years ago.

The next time you are tempted to use a cliché, think for a minute. Picture what you're trying to say in a different way. Figure out your own way of looking at something or getting your point across. If you can, you're on your way to opening your creative side, developing your style, and thinking for yourself. If you're lucky, your brilliant phrase will catch on and become so overused it ends up as tomorrow's cliché.

Shun Run-On Sentences

Do you remember the run-on sentence from the punctuation chapter (section 3-8)? They aren't necessarily long sentences, but individual sentences bashed together without the proper punctuation.

You know how to handle these critters; decide which punctuation works best for your sentence. Choose either a period, semicolon, dash, colon, or a coordinating conjunction.

Sidestep Prepositional Series

I'm all for prepositions. They are useful words. But (and you knew a *but* was coming) avoid too many prepositional phrases in a row. They can make your writing clunky and confusing. When you find your sentences full of prepositional phrases, it's time to rewrite. Perhaps your sentence needs to be two sentences.

> Aardvark placed his book bag <u>on</u> the top shelf <u>in</u> his locker <u>after</u> his last class <u>before</u> he left <u>for</u> the day. (yuck!)

> <u>Before</u> he left school, Aardvark placed his book bag <u>on</u> the top shelf <u>of</u> his locker. (better)

Dodge the Misplaced Modifiers

Modifiers, whether they're one word or a phrase, should be as close as possible to the word or phrase they are describing. If you're not sure of all the different kinds of modifiers, check out the sentence chapter (section 2-18) for a refresher course.

> Clinging to her umbrella, the rain and wind whipped
> (misplaced modifier)   (subject)
> around Grammar Girl.

Oh no! Rain and wind cling to Grammar Girl's umbrella? Do they use Velcro?

> Clinging to her umbrella, Grammar Girl braved the rain and wind whipping around her. (makes much more sense!)

Don't Modify Absolutes

While we're on the topic of modifiers (and we already know about *so* and *very*), I want to discuss some phrases that are dead wrong: modifying words that have absolute meanings, such as *dead* and *unique*.

> That is a very unique painting. (wrong)

The word *unique* means "one of a kind." It's an absolute. Something can't be "more unique" than something else.

> That is the most unique painting I've ever seen.
> (also wrong)

You can use plenty of other words to talk about degrees. A piece of art can be the most stunning painting you've ever seen or very unusual. There's no reason to assign a new meaning to *unique*.

Dead is another absolute word that people use (but shouldn't) with a modifier.

> He was <u>completely</u> and <u>absolutely</u> dead.

You can't be more dead than dead—there are no degrees to deadness, so you shouldn't qualify it.

Quash Those Qualifiers

Other unnecessary words sneak into people's writing. I'm talking about **qualifiers** or modifiers that don't add anything to what they are describing.

Qualifiers are words such as *just, a bit, sort of, almost* (unless you specifically mean almost), *actual, pretty* (as in **pretty much**), *little* (unless you mean size), *even, really*, and *rather*, to name a few.

I'm guilty of overusing *just*.

> If you just write what you really mean instead of pretty much avoiding the actual ideas, your writing will even be a little better. Actually writing sort of what you mean will almost always rather strengthen the sense of your sentence a bit. (yikes!)

> If you write what you mean instead of avoiding the ideas, your writing will be better. Writing what you mean will strengthen the sense of your sentence. (better)

Qualifiers have their place, but make sure they're not just taking up space.

Negate Double Negatives

You know the saying two wrongs don't make a right? If you remember that, you can easily remember not to have two negatives in your sentence.

Squiggly <u>doesn't never</u> eat squash.
(Nope, that means he does eat squash.)

Squiggly <u>doesn't</u> eat squash. (yup)

Squiggly <u>never</u> eats squash. (yup)

When you're writing, choose which negative word best fits in your sentence.

It's easy to spot most negatives—*not, none, never, nothing,* and *no*. But there are a few surprising ones—*hardly, barely,* and *scarcely*.

Squiggly <u>doesn't hardly</u> ever eat squash. (nope)
Squiggly <u>hardly</u> ever eats squash. (yup)

Negativity

While we're on the subject of negatives, use negative sentences sparingly.

Isn't it more helpful when I explain what to do instead of what not to do? It's the same with your sentences.

If you can rewrite a sentence and make it positive—but say what you need to—it's stronger. Save your negative sentences to make a point. If you use negatives sparingly, they will be more powerful.

<u>Don't forget</u> to run your work through your computer's spell-checking tool. (negative)

Run your work through your computer's spell-checking tool. (positive)

Aardvark <u>didn't park close enough</u> to the curb. (negative)

Aardvark parked too far from the curb. (positive)

ACCENTUATE THE POSITIVE

I've spent a lot of time on what not to do and what to watch out for. Here are some tips for what to do.

Choose Your Words with Care

It's easy to write any old sentence.

> He went to the store.

But stronger writers think about their word choices.

Pick strong, concise nouns and verbs that say exactly what you mean. Notice how the sentence develops as I become more specific with my noun and verb choices.

> He went to the store. (What kind of store?)

> He went to the supermarket. (Who went?)

> Squiggly went to the supermarket. (How did Squiggly get there?)

> Squiggly ran to the supermarket.

Although not the most exciting sentence in the world, the last one is specific about who went where and how.

You'd have a different sentence if I used other nouns or verbs.

> Squiggly limped to the drugstore.
> Squiggly raced to the bookstore.

Squiggly's busy, isn't he?

What if the noun isn't a name, but an object?

> The thing that bothered her about him was his habit.

The reader is left asking what habit, why did he do it, how did it bother her, and what did she do when she was bothered?

> When he snapped his fingers continuously while reading, his sister longed to rip the book out of his hands.

This sentence gives you detail—you know his habit (without even saying the word *habit*), their relationship, and what she wants to do. You now have a connection to these two people that you didn't have from the first sentence.

Nouns and verbs drive a sentence, animating your writing. Yet adjectives and adverbs are equally important. They, too, should be chosen with care to mean exactly what you want, but use them sparingly. It's easier to write a string of adjectives, hoping that the combination will get your point across, than it is to choose the perfect descriptor.

> Grammar Girl's dog was so willful and stubborn that Aardvark couldn't walk him.

Rather than write *willful and stubborn*, use your imagination (or your thesaurus) to find the one word that means willful and stubborn. Will *stubborn* suffice? Would *obstinate* or *contrary* be better? The adjective you choose will tell the reader more about the dog.

If your writing seems vague, examine your verbs, nouns, adjectives, and adverbs. Make them work hard. Make each one count.

Show Is Better Than Tell

Good writing, particularly good fiction writing, draws an image in the reader's mind instead of just telling the reader what to think or believe.

> Mr. Bobweave was a fat, ungrateful old man. (boring; simply tells the reader the basics about Mr. Bobweave)

> Mr. Bobweave heaved himself out of the chair. As his feet spread under his weight and his arthritic knees popped

and cracked in objection, he pounded the floor with his cane while cursing that dreadful child who was late again with his coffee. (better; paints a picture in the reader's imagination of a fat, ungrateful old man)

BREAK IT UP

The sentences of a paper or story are grouped into paragraphs; each paragraph represents an idea. The topic sentence contains your main point, which can come at the beginning, middle, or end of your paragraph. The other sentences in the paragraph support the topic statement or further develop the idea.

Make sure your paragraph stays on topic; don't let sentences sneak in that wander in new directions. If you're introducing a new idea or point, you need a new paragraph with its own topic sentence.

New paragraphs should flow smoothly from previous paragraphs. Sometimes you'll use similar words to tie them together (as I used *sentences* near the end of the first paragraph in this section and near the beginning of the second paragraph), and sometimes you'll use connecting words, such as *in addition, furthermore, similarly, however, meanwhile, therefore*, and *on the other hand*, to transition between paragraphs. Other times the topics will be related enough that you won't need special transition elements.

Paragraphs can vary in length, but long paragraphs are generally harder to read than short paragraphs. When writing online or in narrow newsprint columns, it is especially important to keep your paragraphs short.

HOW LONG IS TOO LONG? THE LENGTH OF YOUR SENTENCES

Can you imagine having the same dinner every night? How would you feel if you owned only seven identical outfits, one for each day of the week? What if you still had the same hairstyle you wore when you were five?

Wouldn't you be bored?

If all your sentences are identical in length and construction, your readers could become bored by the sameness.

Your sentences should follow a pattern: 80 words, 265 words, 20 words. Repeat. Just kidding! There is no one perfect length or pattern; you want to weave sentences of different styles and lengths together.

If your sentences are too long, your readers will struggle. Some writers might be able to keep their readers' interest no matter how long the sentence, but if you add too many clauses, put in lots of conjunctions, or add punctuation to keep the sentence going, your reader might forget what the main point of the sentence was, forget how it started, or be unable to follow your ideas. Here's an example of a 198-word sentence based loosely on a passage from a book by Marcel Proust:

Then, at the risk of a horrible stomach ache if he ate too much, or of insomnia from all the caffeine that would build up in his system, as soon as the coast was clear, Squiggly tiptoed to the refrigerator to grab the chocolate cake; while in the dining room, past the hallway and the den, both of them dark, the curtains were closed to keep out the night, and to the left, past the stairs where one would ascend to the bedrooms, Squiggly could sense the monstrous black statue of Sir Fragalot to be watching, whose beady eyes did not sleep at night, a majestic statue yet an ominous one, the embodiment of chivalry, of poor sentence structure, and of the men from the neighboring village who set the peeves squawking and the ladies staring as they approached the schoolhouse on summer nights, when they came to class in their armor, and who, on their way home, just after they had emerged from the shadow of the entrance where so many students entered and endeavored to learn the mysteries of the English language, waved at the townsfolk as though they didn't have a care in the world.

If you actually read the whole thing, you know that it took an enormous amount of concentration; and if you didn't read the whole thing, you know how challenging a long sentence can be. Do your readers a favor and keep your sentences a manageable length.

On the other hand, is your sentence short? too short? too choppy? a fragment? It might have a subject. It might have a verb. It might be a sentence. Is it enough? Are you annoyed? Should I stop? Read on.

Long, convoluted sentences can make it hard for your audience to follow your ideas and logic. Choppy sentences can frazzle them. You want medium-length as well as long and short ones.

Write straightforward sentences that start with the subject. Throw in some sentences that begin with subordinating conjunctions (see section 1-38). And if you're feeling really confident and your writing can be informal, start a couple of sentences with one of the FANBOYS (see section 1-36 and Appendix section A-3). Make sure they're complete sentences, not fragments.

Fixing Sentence Lengths

If your sentences are too short, expand on the details or combine a couple of points. (Use the FANBOYS to join your thoughts.) If you've overdone the fragments, turn them into sentences by making sure you have a subject and verb.

On the other hand, if you've squeezed all your points into one sentence, you need to break it up. First, figure out the main points; you probably have two or three ideas twisted together. Chop it into manageable bits, turning each of your points into its own medium-sized sentence. Make sure the new sentences flow into each other.

The sentence (and ultimately your paper, letter, or story) needs to be interesting, lively, and engaging.

OVERCOMING WRITER'S BLOCK

Some days it just doesn't come together. You stare at the computer screen but can't think of a thing to say. Or maybe you write, but you hate what you've written. Anything you do to overcome writer's block is just a mind game. I don't mean that in a bad way because sometimes you have to play mind games to get your work done. Writing is a solitary experience; it's really all about you and your mind. Here are some things that work for me:

- **Don't play.** If you're going to procrastinate, force yourself to do something productive. Your choices are cleaning your room or writing, doing chores or writing—not playing computer games or writing.

  Some people may advise you to take short, timed play breaks, but that doesn't work for me. If I start playing, I can't stop. If I know I can do something easy instead of writing, I'll opt for the easy thing every time. Sometimes overcoming writer's block means forcing yourself to put in the time.

- **Skip around.** Don't get too fixated on writing the first sentence or paragraph. If you have a great quote or fact, and it falls in the middle of your paper, write that first and come back to the beginning later.

- **Try free writing.** Write without stopping for thirty minutes. It doesn't matter what you write as long as you write. This exercise will show you that you can write, and it will get your juices flowing. A possible bonus is that you might come up with some great thoughts for your paper or great story ideas.

- **Use real deadlines.** Nothing focuses the mind like a deadline. Maybe create a deadline earlier than the real one. That way you'll definitely fit in editing and rewriting time. Plan a treat for yourself when you finish your paper and a bonus if you finish earlier than scheduled. (Put someone else in charge of doling out the treat.)

PROOFREADING TIPS

You are not alone—everyone makes typos (silly mistakes that you didn't catch).

It's nearly impossible to accurately proofread your own writing. Typos are bad and can get you in trouble, but even though you should do your best to catch them, I also think it's important not to beat yourself up too badly when typos happen. Human error is inevitable. The real key to avoiding typos is to have someone else proofread your work. Since that's not always possible, here are some other solutions.

1. **While you're writing on your computer, use the auto-correct feature.** I also call this the "know thyself" trick. For example, I always type *pateint* instead of *patient*. Always. But with the auto-correct feature in my word-processing software, I can tell the computer that every time I type *pateint* it should insert *patient*. Problem solved!

2. **Run your work through your computer's spell-checking tool.** It won't find every error—it won't catch an *it's* that shouldn't have an apostrophe, for example—but it will find words that are flat-out wrong. Consider all the alternatives it suggests; the first choice won't always be the correct choice. It would be embarrassing to have the word *wetter* instead of *whether*. Also the computer's grammar checker isn't always correct. Consider

what it's telling you, but do a little research if its suggestion doesn't seem to make sense.

3. **Once you're finished using the computer's tools, print out your work.** Many people find that if they try to proofread on a computer monitor, they miss more errors than when reading a printed copy.

4. **Give yourself some time.** If possible, let your work sit for a while before you proofread it. If you are able to clear your mind and approach the writing from a fresh perspective, then your brain is more able to focus on the actual words, rather than seeing the words you think you wrote.

5. **Read your work out loud.** This forces you to read each word individually and increases the odds you'll find a typo. Reading your work out loud also lets you hear the rhythm of your sentences and the logic of your thoughts. This is a great method for editing and rewriting.

6. **Force yourself to view every word.** If you don't want to read out loud, you can use the tip of a pencil or pen to physically touch each word. You can also focus on smaller sections of the document by putting a ruler under each line of text as you are reading or by cutting out a small rectangular window on an index card and sliding it over your copy as you read.

7. **Read your work backward,** starting with the last sentence and working your way in reverse order to the beginning. Supposedly, this works better than reading through from the beginning because your brain knows what you meant to write, and you tend to skip over spelling mistakes when you're reading forward.

8. **Make your computer read to you.** Most word-processing software includes a text-to-speech feature that will read your writing to you. It's there for the visually impaired, but you can also harness it for proofreading. Put on headphones and listen to a lovely robotic voice reading your masterpiece. You won't find homophone errors such as *it's* for *its*, but missing or mangled words will jump out at you. (Search for "text to speech" in your software's Help section.)

THE MUSIC OF WRITING

Your ear is the greatest asset in composing sentences, paragraphs, and papers. Grammar is important, but the rhythm of your writing brings the meaning and action of a sentence to the reader. As you read your work, give yourself over to how it sounds. Are the sentences choppy, or do you have some long and short ones interwoven? Do your paragraph breaks come at natural spots, or are they too long or too short?

It's all practice and it isn't always easy, so don't be discouraged. Be impressed with yourself for even paying attention to the rhythm, sounds, and color of your writing.

READING, EDITING, AND REWRITING

Remember when I said to ignore everything until after you wrote your first draft? I meant it.

But once your first draft is done, it's time to edit and rewrite. You might be shocked to learn how many times some professional writers rewrite their work.

Use the following list of what to look for as you edit your work and rewrite. Writers go through different stages—the idea, outlines, research, drafts, edits, rewrites—many times.

Make this guide fit you and how you work.

1. Check spelling through your computer and by reading your work.

2. Check your punctuation. If you're not sure, look up the rules.

3. Check the parts of speech. Are the nouns and verbs agreeing? Are the verb tenses OK? Are you using adjectives and adverbs properly? Do the pronouns agree, and are they clearly representing the nouns they need to? Any dangling modifiers?

4. Are your nouns and verbs precise? Are your adjectives and adverbs necessary, and if so, are they exactly the ones you want?

5. Is most of your writing in the active voice?

6. Check for unnecessary words and phrases. Check for repetition in sentences. Then in paragraphs. Is everything stated as clearly as possible? Are there too many prepositional phrases in a row? Do you have too many "There are" sentences?

7. Any unnecessary qualifiers? Double negatives? Negative sentences that can be rewritten more strongly in a positive way?

8. Did you avoid clichés? Did you present your writing in the style necessary (formal versus informal)? Is there any slang that doesn't belong?

9. Do you have extra-long sentences that are repetitive? Don't say exactly what you mean? Can be divided into two shorter sentences?

10. Do you have choppy sentences that could be joined together with conjunctions or adverbial phrases?

11. Do you have parallel structure within your sentences?

12. Are your paragraph breaks sensible?

13. Does your logic make sense? Is your paper following a logical progression? Did you include everything you need to cover your subject?

14. How does your writing sound? Does it have a rhythm? Read it aloud to check the music of your writing and to spot any typos you might have missed.

15. Did you congratulate yourself?

16. Can you take some time away from your work? If so, wait and then read it again, going through the checklist before your next rewrite.

IS GRAMMAR IMPORTANT WHEN YOU TEXT? IM? E-MAIL?

Of course, I believe grammar is always important—my name is Grammar Girl.

But as you know by now, I am flexible about some things, and I'm an appropriate-to-the-situation kind of Grammar Girl.

So what rules apply when you send e-mail, text, or instant messages?

Formal or Informal: Tuxedo or Jeans?

Whenever I think about language rules, I consider whether a situation is formal or informal. For example, people have asked me if it's OK to start a sentence with a conjunction like *and* or *but*. My answer is that it's OK in informal settings but should be avoided in formal settings.

Be aware of the purpose of your writing. For whom are you writing?

A formal setting is something like a report for school or a letter for a job.

An informal setting is something like a text, e-mail, or instant message to a friend.

A semiformal setting is something like a thank-you note or e-mail to your grandmother. Semiformal is a gray area where you have to use your judgment.

You can see that the answer for formality or informality depends on what you're writing, to whom you're writing, and your relationship with the person. Texting your friend is different from e-mailing your uncle.

Audience Awareness

Just as stand-up comedians need to know their audience to choose the right language, you need to know who your reader is when you're writing an e-mail, text, or instant message.

Your best friend? Text and IM* however you want—you have your own language with your friends.

Your mother? Informal, but remember, she is your mother.

Your grandmother? Does she even have a computer or a cell phone? Would she get what *ROFL* means? Does she prefer a paper note or an e-mail message?

*Some people don't like it when **text** and **e-mail** are used as verbs because they are really modifiers that describe what kind of message you are sending, but it's becoming more acceptable to use the words that way. The Associated Press already considers it standard.

Here are some handy-dandy guidelines for writing e-mail, text, and instant messages to people who aren't your friends:

1. **Think of your reader.** You wouldn't begin an e-mail message to a teacher or an adult neighbor with "Hey, dude"—please, tell me you wouldn't!

    Neither would you write to your grandmother "Thanks for the GR8 boots. MWAH."

    Would your grandmother understand that? Maybe, but probably not. If your reader can't understand you, then don't bother writing in the first place.

    How you write to your friends is one thing, but when you write to an adult in your personal life (relative, teacher, or family friend) or for a job or internship, you have to think about what that person will understand.

    Some people would consider it rude to use text-messaging abbreviations when the person on the receiving end won't understand them. It may also be rude not to use them when you are sending a message to someone you know will understand the abbreviations and is reading your message on a tiny cell phone screen.

    It's OK to use abbreviations with your friends, but think twice when writing to others.

2. **What's it all about?** I have received countless e-mail messages that bear no relation to the subject line. Or there's no subject listed at all. That drives me crazy.

    Alert your reader to what the message is about.

    If you need information about your upcoming trip, write "Visit in August" or "Camping" in the subject line. It's polite and clues in your readers before they read the message.

    The Quick and Dirty Tip is to make sure your subject line

matches the message content. This is especially true if you're writing about a job or an internship.

3. **The body of the e-mail.** When writing to adults or superiors, be polite (not that you shouldn't be polite to your friends, but you know there is a difference).

   If it's a somewhat informal e-mail and it's acceptable to use the person's first name, start with "Hi, John," (notice the commas—see section 3-8).

   If it's more formal, you might want to write "Dear John," or "Dear Mr. Henderson," (use a comma after the name).

   Use correct grammar. It's very impressive—honestly. Write sentences. Unless it's a friend or close relative who understands, don't use abbreviations.

   Don't write in all caps—in e-mail talk, that's shouting. Use uppercase and lowercase letters. Not capitalizing the first letter in a sentence makes you look lazy.

4. **Content.** In the first couple of lines, say what the e-mail is about. If you're in charge of arranging carpooling to rehearsals, write that in the first paragraph. People skim e-mail messages, so it's good to get to the point quickly.

   If you're writing to parents, you may want to start with "Thanks for helping me arrange the rides for rehearsal." You're easing into the subject by thanking them right away and letting them know the subject of the message.

   Polite, informative, and grammatically correct—ooh la la!

5. **Formatting.** Keep your messages short—unless you use e-mail to write personal letters.

   Most people prefer to read short e-mail messages. Try to keep it to a few paragraphs.

Use paragraph breaks; it makes messages easier to read.

6. **Proofread.** It's easy to make mistakes. Use the spell-check tool and then make sure that you picked the right correction.

   Spell-check doesn't always know when you leave out a word (and that can change the meaning). Leaving out *not* in the following sentence changes the kind of clothes you should wear to a carnival:

   > I'm willing to volunteer for the water-dunking event.

   Suppose you really meant to write

   > I'm <u>not</u> willing to volunteer for the water-dunking event.

7. **Where is the unsend button?** There is usually no unsend button for e-mail or text messages. If you've written something angry or mean, think before you send it!

   If you're really angry or hurt, wait a day before hitting that send button. You can't get the message back.

   Also, it would be nice to think that your message will be seen only by the person you are writing to; nice, but not always realistic. E-mail messages get forwarded, and people accidentally hit "Reply All" instead of "Reply."

   Again, it's important to consider your reader. Since readers can't see or hear you, they won't know if you're joking or serious. E-mail messages don't convey tone or facial expressions. If you think something might not come off as you meant it, consider rewriting or communicating in person. Think of your reader's feelings.

   Before you hit "Send," imagine how you would feel if your message were posted on the school wall or shown to your mom.

LETTER WRITING

At some time you may have to write a letter. You may even want to. Letters that you send by snail mail require a slightly different form than e-mails—and I don't just mean that they're on paper.

A Business Letter

If you're writing a letter for a job, include your name, address, phone number, and e-mail address at the top of the letter so that the recipient can contact you. Be sure to use a professional-sounding e-mail address. Nobody wants to hire smellyboy@noreply.com. Also include the date and the name and address of the person you're writing to.

Then begin the letter with a **salutation**—the phrase of greeting that comes before the body of the letter. If it's a letter about a job, you probably won't be on a first-name basis, so you need to write *Mr.* or *Ms.* If you're not sure whether it's a man or a woman, write the person's whole name. In a business letter, use a colon after the salutation.

The body of the letter—what you want to tell the person—comes next. You probably want to make a good impression on this person, so pay attention to grammar, sentence structure, word choices, and spelling.

At the end of the body of the letter, add the sign-off, the phrase that closes it. *Sincerely* is a good formal sign-off for business letters to people you don't know well or don't correspond with often. Always place a comma after the sign-off. Because you've placed your name on the top of the letter, just sign the bottom and you're done.

May 18, 2015

Mr. Nice Person
Terrific Company
456 Wayward Way
East Eden, Alaska 99999

Dear Mr. Person:

[Body of letter]

Sincerely,
Grammar Girl

Informal Letters

You can follow the business format if you'd like, but it isn't necessary when writing a letter to a relative. Informal letters are more free-form and simple.

You should date your letter. You probably want to include the recipient's name, but in an informal letter, you can use a comma after the name. After you finish the body of the letter (what you're actually saying), sign off. It could be as personal as *Love* or as general as *Best* or *Yours truly*. Again, a comma follows the sign-off.

After you sign your name, you might have an afterthought or a comment that doesn't relate to the main message of your letter.

PS is an abbreviation for the Latin words *post scriptum*, which mean "after writing." The PS has traditionally been used to add a thought after the writer has finished the main body of a letter.

Although it is common to see additional levels of *PS*s written as *PSS* and *PSSS*, the correct way to write it is *PPS* (*post post scriptum*) and *PPPS* (*post post post scriptum*). You decide how many *PS*s your grandfather will tolerate.

May 18, 2015

Dear Uncle Joe,

[Body of letter]

Love and kisses,
Grammar Girl

PS Did I mention that I'm writing a book?

THE END OF THE BOOK, BUT THE BEGINNING FOR YOU

I hope I've given you the tools you need to write with confidence. I think of grammar and usage as the rules to the game of writing, and the rules are just the building blocks of creativity. Writing proper sentences doesn't ensure that your work will be inspiring, but it can keep errors from marring your brilliance.

Never let fear of making mistakes keep you from writing. Just do your best. Forget about the rules in your first draft and revise later. Look up things if you don't know them. If something wasn't covered in this book (the Appendix also has lots of extra informtion), you can likely find it in a dictionary, usage guide, or style guide.

If someone marks up your writing with a big red pen, consider it a learning experience and go on.

If nothing else, write your grandmother a letter that will make her proud.

Writing well is one of the secrets to being taken seriously. Learning the rules and suggestions in this book will give you confidence and help you continue on a path of success. If you communicate clearly, people will be less likely to dismiss your ideas just because you're young. Writing well is like riding a bike or swimming—once you get the basics down, you can do it for the rest of your life—but you can also continue to fine-tune your skills, getting better with practice as the years go by.

Appendix

SPECIFIC CAPITALIZATION RULES

WHAT IS IN A NAME?

Nicknames are capitalized, but terms of endearment are not. A nickname is a specific, alternative name for someone. A term of endearment can be used for anyone; it's not specific to an individual.

Everyone calls my little sister Honey because she's so sweet.
"It's you and me, honey."

The same rule holds true for family names such as *mother*, *mom*, *father*, and *dad*.

Say hi to your <u>mother</u> for me. (*Mother* is a generic descriptor.)
Say hi to <u>Mom</u> for me. (*Mom* is like her name in this sentence.)
You're driving me crazy, <u>Mother</u>. (*Mother* is used as her name in this sentence.)

Aunt, *uncle*, and *cousin* are also usually lowercase unless they are part of someone's name.

Did you call <u>Aunt Mathilda</u>?
My <u>aunt</u>, Mathilda, always hiccups during dinner.

I know relatives can be difficult at times, but at least now when you're complaining about your siblings or parents, you can do it in a grammatically correct way! Isn't that always a plus?

PLACES, EVERYONE

Capitalize the names of cities, states, countries, counties, and other specific places such as oceans, streets, rivers, and parks.

> The creek behind my house runs from New Jersey to New York.
> "Mississippi River" has too many vowels in it.

Except That . . .

If you mention two rivers, the word *rivers* (or *oceans*, *mountains*, etc.) is not capitalized.

The Amazon and Hudson rivers never intersect.

Planets

Planet names, such as Mars and Jupiter, are always capitalized because they refer to specific places.

For some reason, most people treat *earth* differently and don't capitalize it. Sometimes you'll see *earth* capitalized when it's listed with all the other planet names or when it's referred to in an astronomical way. For example, it will likely be capitalized in a sentence talking about space travel: "We plan to leave Earth in January and arrive at Mars in October." But it is likely to be lowercased in a sentence where it is used more generically: "I'm wishing for peace on earth and goodwill to men."

Of course, when you are using the word *earth* to refer to dirt, it's lowercased.

Let's not forget the sun and moon. They are not capitalized. Lots of planets have suns and moons, so the words are generic (common nouns) like *bridge* and *expert*.

DIRECTIONS: WANDERING THE FOUR CORNERS OF THE EARTH

Direction names are lowercase when they describe a direction and uppercase when they describe a specific place (just like other proper nouns).

> Go <u>southeast</u> until you reach the mall, then head <u>west</u>.
> He moved from <u>the South</u> to <u>the Midwest</u>.
> The Cannes Film Festival is held in <u>southern France</u>.
> Almost everyone in <u>South Korea</u> buys ringtones.

TIME TO CAP: DAYS, MONTHS, HOLIDAYS, AND SEASONS

Days of the week, names of months, and holidays are capitalized, but seasons are lowercased (unless they are part of a proper name).

> Last <u>November</u> we had the <u>winter</u> dance on a <u>Friday</u>.
> The <u>2010 Winter Olympics</u> were in Vancouver.
> Thanksgiving is my favorite <u>fall</u> holiday.

AWARD NAMES

Formal award names (such as Oscar, Grammy, and Nobel Prize) are capitalized because they are proper nouns—the names of specific things. General award terms are not capitalized when they are used descriptively.

> Who will win a <u>Pulitzer Prize</u> this year?
> Amy Winehouse won five <u>Grammys</u>.
> Doris Lessing won a <u>Nobel Prize</u> in 2007.
> Doris Lessing won a literature <u>prize</u>.
> Squiggly won the school writing <u>award</u>.

RELIGIONS AND NATIONALITIES: BEING POLITE

When referring to people of a specific religion or nationality, the words are capitalized: Christians, Muslims, Jews, Sikhs, African Americans, Native Americans, Dutch, Germans, etc.

When a country graciously gives its name to a specific thing, such as a type of food or an illness, you usually use caps—German measles, Spanish rice, and Japanese noodles.

The same is true for most words derived from proper nouns such as *Kafkaesque* (from the name of the author Franz Kafka) and *Darwinian* (from the name of the scientist Charles Darwin)—they are capitalized. Check a dictionary, though, before you automatically capitalize such words.

RELIGIOUS TERMS: GOD BLESS GRAMMAR GIRL

Following the rules for any other proper noun, capitalize *god* when it is the name of one specific god in any religion. When the word refers to multiple gods or is a description, it is lowercased.

> Different religions have different names for a supreme being, including Jehovah, Allah, Yahweh, and God.
>
> Stories about the Greek gods provide great inspiration for modern fiction.
>
> The god Apollo is often shown playing the lyre.

The names of religions such as Christianity and Islam are also capitalized; the names of religious texts such as the Bible and the Koran are often capitalized.

DEGREES AND DEPARTMENTS

People often think there is a typo on my "About Grammar Girl" Web page because it says I have an undergraduate degree in English (capitalized) and a graduate degree in biology (lowercased).

Although I've never claimed to be perfect, that isn't a typo. *English* is capitalized because it is derived from a proper noun (*England*), and *biology* is lowercased because it is not derived from a proper noun. Similarly, *Spanish*, *Italian*, and *German* are capitalized and *chemistry*, *math*, and *visual arts* are not.

Department is capitalized when it is part of the exact name of a specific department, but not when it is used generically as a common noun.

> The Department of Computer Gaming issued an announcement.
>
> The department chairperson just won the World of Warcraft pumpkin-carving contest.

The names of degrees usually aren't capitalized.

Aardvark earned a bachelor's degree in ant behavior.
Aardvark received a bachelor of science degree.

YOU'RE ENTITLED TO CAP

In general, formal titles that come before names are capitalized, and formal titles that come after names are not capitalized. The key distinction you have to make is whether the word is part of an official title (in which case it is capitalized) or just describing someone's role (in which case it is lowercased). Common titles include *emperor, president, mayor, director,* and *chairperson.*

We invited President Aardvark to dinner.
Aardvark, the class president, came to dinner.
The president came to dinner.

Sometimes a title may come directly before the name but still be lowercased because it's describing someone's role rather than being part of the name:

Class president Aardvark Blueback came over for dinner.

Similarly, if you have the pleasure of addressing a knight, *sir* is capitalized. If you are addressing someone who is not a knight, *sir* is lowercased.

Please, Sir Fragalot, repeat the sentence.
Please repeat the sentence, sir.

BREEDS: WOOF AND MEOW

When in doubt about whether to capitalize a breed name, consult a dictionary, but in general, the rules are the same as for other nouns: capitalize words derived from proper nouns and lowercase words derived from common nouns.

beagle
British shorthair

English mastiff
Havana brown
ragdoll
Yorkshire terrier

THE CAPITOL, THE CONGRESS, AND THE CONSTITUTION

In the United States, when the word *capitol* refers to the specific capitol building in Washington, DC, it is capitalized.

The president walked over to the Capitol.

When it refers to the capitol building of a state or a complex of buildings, it is lowercased: *capitol.*

The state senators walked to the capitol in Carson City after lunch.

When it's part of the name of a specific neighborhood, it's also capitalized:

I have fond memories of Seattle's Capitol Hill neighborhood.

Similarly, *Congress* is capitalized when it refers to the U.S. Senate and House of Representatives or a specific session of the U.S. legislative body:

He spoke before the 22nd Congress.
He's speaking before Congress today.

The adjective *congressional* is lowercased.

The word *Constitution* is capitalized when it is used to refer to the United States Constitution. However, the adjective *constitutional* is lowercased. The names of other historical documents, treaties, proclamations, bills, and acts are also capitalized: *Magna Carta, Treaty of Versailles, Declaration of Independence, First Amendment, Bill of Rights, Patriot Act*, and so on.

THE WORD *THE*

Whether you capitalize *the* in titles is a matter of style. *The New York Times Manual of Style and Usage* recommends using a capital *the* in names of newspapers, journals, and magazines when you write them in a sentence, but *The Chicago Manual of Style* recommends using a lowercase *the* in the same situation. Since the titles of both style guides start with *the*, I can't discern any bias.

I recommend following a specific style guide or, if you're writing the name of a newspaper or magazine, check how they handle it themselves and follow their lead.

THE INTERNET—A CAPITAL IDEA!

Words are capitalized because they are proper nouns, not because they are important or new.

When you talk about the Internet, there is only one thing you could be referring to—so *Internet* is a proper noun and gets capitalized.

Web, which is short for "World Wide Web," is also generally considered to be one specific thing, so it also gets capitalized.

On the other hand, *Web site* or *website* is trickier. There are hundreds of millions of websites on the Web. If you use the open compound (*Web site*), the Web part gets capitalized, because *Web* is still a proper noun, but *site* is not. If you close the compound (*website*), the entire word is a common noun because it is not a name for one specific thing, so it is lowercased.

Whether you use the open or closed compound is a matter of style. If your teacher has a preference, that's the way to go. I like *website.*

WE'RE NOT FINISHED YET

Remember this Quick and Dirty Tip?

specific noun = caps
general noun = lowercase

But there are exceptions, and some words are less clear. With some words, you have to decide whether they are naming something specific or something general. (And even then, sometimes the answer isn't clear, so you just have to use your best judgment.)

For example, *depression* is sometimes a proper noun and sometimes a common noun. If you're talking about a general economic depression or medical condition, then it's lowercased; but if you're talking about the Great Depression, then you are referring to a specific historical period, so it's capitalized.

Traditionally, *ground zero* means the site of a nuclear explosion, and sometimes it is used to refer to the site of a more general explosion or an area where rapid change has taken place. In those general instances, *ground zero* would be a common noun and wouldn't be capitalized. But, since September 2001, the name Ground Zero has been assigned to the site of the World Trade Center in New York. When used so specifically, it becomes a proper noun that needs to be capitalized.

Note that as in other cases, the specificity turns these general nouns into proper nouns.

A-2 CONJUNCTIVE ADVERBS

Conjunctive adverbs are transitional words that join two clauses that could be independent sentences. Use a semicolon before the conjunctive adverb to join two clauses. (See Chapter Four for a discussion of using *however* as a conjunctive adverb.) Examples of words that can be used as conjunctive adverbs include the following:

accordingly	hence	next
again	however	nonetheless
also	incidentally	otherwise
anyway	indeed	similarly
besides	instead	specifically
certainly	likewise	still
consequently	meanwhile	subsequently
finally	moreover	then
further	namely	therefore
furthermore	nevertheless	thus

CONJUNCTIONS

FANBOYS

Coordinating conjunctions are the little words you use to join other parts of speech. They can join subjects, objects, modifiers, phrases, and clauses.

F—for
A—and
N—nor
B—but
O—or
Y—yet
S—so

SUBORDINATING CONJUNCTIONS

Subordinating conjunctions join subordinate clauses to other clauses. The following is a list of common subordinating conjunctions:

after	how	that
although	if	though
as	lest	unless
as if	now that	until
as in	once	when
as long as	provided	whenever
because	rather than	where
before	since	whereas
despite	so that	whether
even though	than	while

VERBS

LINKING VERBS

A linking verb can also be called a **copula**.

The Complete Conjugation of *To Be*

To be is always a linking verb.

> *be (am, are, is, was, were, have been, has been, had been, will be, will have been, would be, would have been)*

COMMON IRREGULAR VERBS

Regular verbs take their past-tense form by adding *d* or *ed*. Irregular verbs don't follow these typical conjugation rules. Here are some of the common irregular verbs:

Present Tense	Past Tense	Present Tense	Past Tense
arise	arose	cut	cut
awake	awoke	deal	dealt
be	was, were	dig	dug
begin	began	do	did
bend	bent	draw	drew
bet	bet	drink	drank
bind	bound	drive	drove
bite	bit	eat	ate
bleed	bled	fall	fell
blow	blew	feed	fed
break	broke	feel	felt
breed	bred	lay	laid
bring	brought	lie	lay
build	built	lose	lost
burst	burst	make	made
buy	bought	mean	meant
cast	cast	meet	met
catch	caught	mislead	misled
choose	chose	mistake	mistook
cling	clung	overcome	overcame
come	came	overdo	overdid
cost	cost	overdraw	overdrew
creep	crept	overtake	overtook

Present Tense	Past Tense	Present Tense	Past Tense
overthrow	overthrew	set	set
pay	paid	shake	shook
put	put	shed	shed
quit	quit	sing	sang
read	read	teach	taught
rid	rid	tell	told
ride	rode	think	thought
rise	rose	throw	threw
run	ran	thrust	thrust
say	said	tread	trod
see	saw	understand	understood
seek	sought	uphold	upheld
sell	sold	upset	upset
send	sent	wake	woke

ADJECTIVES

GETTING BOSSY WITH ADJECTIVES (ORDERING THEM AROUND)

Most people who grow up speaking English put adjectives in the proper order in sentences without giving it much thought. In fact, many of you will probably be surprised to learn that there is a quasi-official proper order. Surprise!

Adjectives should go in the following order, with opinion first and purpose last:

Opinion (ridiculous, crazy, beautiful)

Size (big, small)

Age (old, young)

Shape (round, square)

Color (yellow, blue)

Origin (American, British)

Material (polyester, styrofoam)

Purpose (swimming, as in *swimming pool*; shooting, as in *shooting range*)

The first letters of the words spell something that almost sounds like a word: OSASCOMP.

These are examples of sentences with the adjectives in the standard order:

Squiggly's <u>crazy, big</u> idea stunned the audience.
(opinion, size)

Aardvark threw his <u>old, round wooden</u> ball at Squiggly.
(age, shape, material)

Grammar Girl wanted to swim in the <u>small blue swimming</u> pool.
(size, color, purpose)

A DASH OF THIS, A DASH OF THAT: DIFFERENT TYPES OF DASHES

A-6

You may have heard of two different kinds of dashes: em dashes (—) and en dashes (-). An em dash is longer than an en dash. Those may seem like strange names, but historically the em dash was as long as the width of a capital typeset letter M, and the en dash was as long as the width of a capital typeset letter N. Now with computer typesetting, the width of an en dash always falls midway between a hyphen and an em dash.

The em dash is the kind of dash I was referring to in section 3-16; it is the kind of dash you use in a sentence. When people say "Use a dash," they almost always mean the em dash.

How can Fran—the love of my life—leave me?

The en dash is used much less frequently and usually only to indicate a range of inclusive numbers. You would use an en dash to write something like this:

Squiggly will be on vacation December 2 through December 9.
Squiggly will be on vacation December 2–December 9.

The *through* and the en dash between the dates indicate that Squiggly will not be in the office starting the second of December and will return on the tenth of December (because an en dash indicates that the numbers are inclusive of those two dates).

Whether you are using the longer em dash in a sentence or the shorter en dash to indicate an inclusive range, it's better to have no spaces between the dash and the surrounding letters.

FORMATTING VERTICAL LISTS

I'm going to discuss vertical lists now. I think you're ready. You've experienced the period, comma, and colon. You know about capitalization. Take a deep breath. This won't hurt.

BULLETS, NUMBERS, AND LETTERS

If you're going to use a list, the first question to ask yourself is what kind of list you should use.

Bullets are just big dots, and you use them when the order of the items doesn't matter. For example, you could use bullets to list the items you want everyone to bring to a beach party.

> I wish I were in Santa Cruz right now. I'd have a party and make s'mores. Everyone would need
>
> - Chocolate bars
> - Graham crackers
> - Marshmallows
> - Pointy sticks

When the order isn't important, I usually list the items alphabetically or in some other way that seems to make sense. The list in the s'mores example is alphabetical, but if my name for the pointy sticks was something that didn't fall at the end alphabetically, I still would have grouped all the food items together and put the sticks at the end. Or you might want to put your most important item first. In Grammar Girl's world, chocolate would always be first, although recipe items are typically written in order of use.

Numbers are reserved for instances where the items in the list need to follow a specific sequence. You could use numbers to list tasks in the order required to start up a piece of machinery.

1. Plug in
2. Turn on power switch
3. Release safety latch
4. Tilt toward Death Star

Letters are useful when you're implying that readers need to choose individual items or when items don't need to follow a specific sequence but you want to refer to an item again later.

Visit the Grammar Girl website for these free extras:

a. Grammar discussions
b. Quizzes
c. An e-mail newsletter

Letters make sense with that list because the order doesn't matter, and I can refer to item b if I want to promote the free quizzes again later.

Remember from section 3-14 about colons that if your lead-in statement is a complete sentence, then you use a colon at the end to introduce your list (as in this example). On the other hand, if your lead-in statement is a sentence fragment, don't use a colon.

Capitalization in Lists

After you've completed the introductory sentence, your next question will be whether to capitalize the first letter in the statements that come after your bullets, numbers, or letters.

If your list item is a complete sentence, capitalize the first letter. If your list item isn't a complete sentence, you can choose whether to capitalize the first letter—it's a style issue. The most important thing is to be consistent (or follow your teacher's guidelines).

Punctuation in Lists

At the end of the first item, you have to decide what kind of punctuation to use.

If your list items are complete sentences, or if at least one list item is a fragment that is immediately followed by a complete sentence, use normal terminal punctuation: a period, question mark, or exclamation point.

For the following reasons, I feel bad for people who don't visit the website:

- They miss the grammar discussions.
- They can't take the free quizzes.
- They can't sign up for the e-mail newsletter that includes free grammar tips.

If your list items are single words or sentence fragments, you can choose whether to use terminal punctuation. Again, the important thing is to be consistent. I don't use terminal punctuation after single words or sentence fragments. I think periods look strange after things that aren't sentences.

The following additional content is available on the website:

- Grammar discussions
- Free quizzes
- A free e-mail newsletter

Finally, your text will be easier to read if you don't put commas or semicolons after the items and don't put a conjunction such as *and* before the last item. They are unnecessary clutter. (If you find yourself really wanting to present your list this way, that probably means you should write it out as a sentence.) Suppose you are thinking of writing it as follows:

The following additional content is available on the website:

- Grammar discussions,
- Free quizzes, and
- A free e-mail newsletter.

Consider instead writing it like this:

The following additional content is available on the website: grammar discussions, free quizzes, and a free e-mail newsletter.

Parallelism

OK, now that you've got the mechanics down for lists, don't forget to be a good writer and make sure all your list items are parallel. That means each list item should be structured the same way. They should all be fragments, or they should all be complete sentences. If you start one bullet point with a verb, start every bullet point with a verb.

For Aardvark, a vacation involves

- Attending lectures
- Reading books
- Seeing sights

Each bullet point is formed the same way—each one starts with a verb.

On the other hand, even though the following list is grammatically correct, it's considered poor writing because the list items aren't parallel.

For Aardvark, a vacation involves

- Attending lectures
- Books
- Many trips to famous destinations

The first item starts with a verb. The next item is a single noun. The third item is a phrase. Choose one form and stay with that form for your list.

Style for Lists

Many of the points I've covered in this section are style issues, meaning that I've run across multiple books and online style guides that make different recommendations. My suggestions are based on what I've studied and on what seems logical to me—for example, writing the items in a bulleted list alphabetically seemed to be the best solution to me. If your teacher has a preference, however, go with that.

CITING A WEBSITE: ARE YOU GOING TO CITE ME FOR THAT?

The purpose of putting citations in your work is to allow other people to see where you got your information and go look at it themselves if they are interested.

Citing a website for a report can be unpredictable. The first thing to find out is whether your teacher accepts websites as sources of information.

If so, you have to determine whether the site is a credible source, and you have to worry about whether it will still exist tomorrow.

Here are a few things to look for and consider when determining if a source is trustworthy:

- Can you tell who wrote the site? If so, does the author seem to have any expertise in the area you are researching? A university website is more credible than Aunt Mary's All Information Page.

- Can you tell when the page you are looking at was written? Something written recently is generally more credible than something that hasn't been updated in years.

- Are there a lot of typos? If there are a lot of language mistakes, it can mean that there are a lot of factual mistakes too.

- Has the website been reviewed by experts; does it bear a seal of approval?

- Does the page cite other credible sources you can check?

- Do other credible sites link to the site? You can find out by doing a specialized search on Google. Enter *link:URL* into the search box. For example, enter *link:www.grammar.quickanddirtytips.com* to find out that libraries, writing centers, universities, teachers, and award sites have linked to the Grammar Girl site, giving it credibility.

Pages disappearing or changing their Web address are problems that are out of your control. If it is an important source, consider printing out the page or saving it on your own computer. If you find that a page is gone and you haven't had a chance to save it yourself, you can sometimes find it at the Internet Archive (also known as the Wayback Machine at www.archive.org).

FORMATTING CITATIONS

There are many different ways to format citations, but they all strive to include these main elements when they are available:

Author
Title
Name of the work (the newspaper, magazine, book, website, etc.)
Work designator (e.g., newspaper or magazine issue and volume)
Publisher
Date of publication
Page number or website address

A-9

SPEAKING VERSUS WRITING, OR FORMAL VERSUS INFORMAL

We all do it. We all speak informally (and sometimes incorrectly), and that's fine in most circumstances. Even I, Grammar Girl, have been known to start a sentence with *hopefully* and utter a few *you know*s.

But you should at least know the right way of speaking and writing. Below are a few examples of the wrong word usually substituted for the right one.

Try to use the right one when you write, and perhaps think about it as you speak—at least if you're speaking in a debate, to a teacher, or at a job interview.

AND VERSUS *TO*

And is a conjunction and *to* is a preposition; they don't serve the same functions in a sentence. Use *to* before a verb—it's part of the verb phrase.

Make sure <u>and</u> download every song I want. (nope)
Make sure <u>to</u> download every song I want. (yup)

HAVE VERSUS OF

Of is not a verb nor is it part of a verb phrase. It's a preposition and shouldn't be used in place of *have*.

> I wish I could <u>of</u> gone to the concert. (nope)
> I wish I could <u>have</u> gone to the concert. (yup)
> If he could <u>of</u>, he would <u>of</u>. (nope)
> If he could <u>have</u>, he would <u>have</u>. (yup)

LIKE VERSUS SUCH AS

Use *like* when your example is similar to what you mean; use *such as* when your example is exactly what you mean.

> She said something <u>like</u> "I'm outta here."
> Squiggly loves sweets, <u>such as</u> cookies and cake.

THIS VERSUS A

Try not to overuse *this*, which is a very specific adjective meaning "right here." *A* is more general.

> Squiggly wanted to buy <u>this</u> computer at the store, but he didn't. (nope)

> Squiggly wanted to buy <u>a</u> computer at the store, but he didn't. (yup)

Quick and Dirty Grammar at a Glance

Sometimes you just need a quick fix.

A/An: Use *a* before consonant sounds; use *an* before vowel sounds. *She has an MBA. It's a Utopian idea.*

Abbreviations (making them plural): Add an *s* (without an apostrophe) to the end of an abbreviation to make it plural. *Smith had two RBIs tonight.*

Affect/Effect: Most of the time *affect* is a verb and *effect* is a noun. *He affected her. The effect mattered.*

A lot/Alot/Allot: *A lot* means "a large number" and is two words, not one. *Allot* means "to parcel out."

Alright/All right: *Alright* is not a standard word. Only use *all right*.

Assure/Ensure/Insure: *Assure* means "to reassure"; *ensure* means "to guarantee"; *insure* refers to insurance.

Because: It's OK to start a sentence with *because*; just be sure you haven't created a sentence fragment. *Because Squiggly was tired, he forgot to stow the chocolate.* (OK) *Because Squiggly was tired.* (wrong)

Between/Among: Use *between* when you are writing about two things and *among* when you are writing about more than two things. There are exceptions, though.

Between you and I/between you and me: *Between you and me* is the correct phrase.

Can/May: Traditionalists maintain that *can* refers to ability and *may* refers to permission. *Can you fix the broken dishwasher? May I go to the mall?*

Capital/Capitol: *Capital* refers to a city, uppercase letter, or wealth. A *capitol* is a building.

Colon: Use a colon in a sentence only after something that would be a complete sentence on its own.

Comma (equals a pause): It is *not* a rule that you put a comma in wherever you would naturally pause in a sentence.

Comma (serial): It's up to you whether to use a serial comma (the comma before the final *and* in a list of items).

Complement/Compliment: Things that work well together complement each other. Compliments are a form of praise.

Dead: *Dead* is an absolute word that shouldn't be modified with words such as *completely* or *very*.

Different from/Different than: In most cases, *different from* is the preferred form.

Each/Every: *Each* and *every* are singular and mean close to the same thing.

E.g./I.e.: *E.g.* means "for example"; *i.e.* means roughly "that is."

E-mail/Email: Both forms are acceptable; traditionalists prefer *e-mail.*

Everyone/Everybody: *Everyone* and *everybody* are singular and mean the same thing.

Farther/Further: *Farther* refers to physical distance; *further* relates to metaphorical distance or means "moreover." *Aardvark ran farther than Squiggly. Further, they hope to run tomorrow.*

Fewer/Less: Use *fewer* for count nouns; use *less* for mass nouns. *He caught fewer fish. The lake had less water.*

Groups (collective nouns): Collective nouns describe a group of things, such as *furniture* and *team*. They are singular in the United States.

Hanged/Hung: People (or animals) who are executed are hanged; everything else is hung.

Historic/Historical: *Historic* is an adjective that means something important or influential in history. *Historical* refers to anything from the past, important or not.

Hopefully: Although it isn't wrong, don't start a sentence with *hopefully*—too many people believe it's wrong.

However: It's OK to start a sentence with *however*, but be careful with your comma placement. *However, we wish he hadn't used permanent ink. However hard Squiggly tried, he couldn't reach the chocolate.*

Hyphen: Never use a hyphen in place of a dash.

Internet: *Internet* is capitalized.

In to/Into: *Into* is a preposition that specifies a direction; sometimes the words *in* and *to* just end up next to each other. *Move into the foyer. We went in to lunch.*

Its/It's: *Its* is the possessive form of *it*; *it's* means "it is" or "it has." *It's a shame the tree lost its leaves.*

Lay/Lie: Objects are laid down; subjects lie down. *I will lay the pen on the table. I want to lie down.*

Literally: *Literally* means "exactly." Don't use it for emphasis or to mean "figuratively."

Log in/Log on/Log out/Log off: These are all acceptable two-word verb phrases. They require a hyphen when used as an adjective. *I want to log in. Please give me the log-in code.*

May/Might: *May* implies more of a likelihood that something is possible than *might. We may go out. Pigs might fly. Might* is also the past tense of *may.*

Modifiers (misplaced): Make sure your modifiers apply to the right words. *I only eat chocolate.* (The only thing I do with chocolate is eat it.) *I eat only chocolate.* (I eat nothing but chocolate.)

Myself: *Please visit Aardvark and myself* is an incorrect hypercorrection. The correct form is *Please visit Aardvark and me.*

Nauseated/Nauseous: *Nauseated* means you feel queasy; *nauseous* describes something that makes you queasy. *The nauseous smell is making me nauseated.*

Numbers (at the beginning of a sentence): Write out numbers at the beginning of a sentence.

Online/On line: *Online* is one word, not two.

Periods (abbreviations at the end of a sentence): Don't use two periods if you have an abbreviation at the end of a sentence.

Periods (with parentheses): Periods go outside parentheses unless what's inside the parentheses is a complete sentence and the parentheses are not within another sentence.

Possession (compound): When two people share something, they share an apostrophe. When two people have separate things, they each need their own apostrophe. *We're at Squiggly and Aardvark's house. Have you met Squiggly's and Aardvark's mothers?*

Possession (words that end with s): The most common way to make a singular word that ends with s possessive is to add a lone apostrophe (*Steve Jobs' keynote*), but it's not wrong to add an s after the apostrophe (*Steve Jobs's keynote*). Some people make the decision based on pronunciation (*Steve Jobs' keynote, Kansas's statute*).

Prepositions (ending sentences with): It's OK to end a sentence with a preposition, except when the preposition is dispensable. *Whom did you step on?* (OK) *Where is he at?* (wrong)

Question marks (with indirect questions): Don't use a question mark after an indirect question. *I wonder why Squiggly left.*

Quotation marks (with other punctuation): Commas and periods go inside quotation marks; colons and semicolons go outside quotation marks. Question marks and exclamation points can go inside or outside quotation marks depending on the context.

Quote/Quotation: *Quote* is a verb; *quotation* is a noun. *I want to quote you. Is this the correct quotation?*

Sentences (run-on): Run-on sentences aren't necessarily long sentences; they are created when main clauses are joined without proper punctuation.

Sit/Set: Subjects sit; objects are set. *I want to sit down. I will set the pen on the table.*

Split infinitives: It's OK to split infinitives. *They want to boldly go where no one has gone before.* Some people, particularly older people, may object.

Subject/Object: The subject in a sentence takes the action; the object receives or is the target of the action. *[Subject] threw the ball. Squiggly threw the [object].*

Than/Then: Use *than* for comparison; use *then* for time. *Aardvark is taller than Squiggly. Then they went fishing.*

That/Which: Use *that* with restrictive clauses; use *which* with nonrestrictive clauses. *I like gems that sparkle, including diamonds, which are expensive.*

That/Who: Use *that* to refer to things; use *who* to refer to people.

Unique: *Unique* is an absolute word that shouldn't be modified with a word such as *most* or *very*.

Verbs (action and linking): Use adverbs to modify action verbs, and adjectives to modify linking verbs. *He ran terribly. He is terrible.*

Was/Were: Use *were* to refer to things that are wishful or not true. *I was at the store. If I were rich, I would buy a yacht.*

Who/Whom: Use *who* to refer to a subject; use *whom* to refer to an object. *Who loves Squiggly? Whom do you love?*

Your/You're: *Your* is the possessive form of *you; you're* means "you are."

Glossary

Aardvark: A blue aardvark, Grammar Girl's friend.

Abbreviation: Any shortened form of a word.

Acronym: A type of abbreviation made from the first letter (or letters) of a string of words, pronounced as if it is a word itself.

Action Verb: A verb that describes actions.

Active Voice: When the action of the verb is performed by the subject of a sentence.

Adjective: A word that describes a noun (or a pronoun) by telling you which one, what kind, or how many.

Adverb: A word that describes a verb, an adjective, other adverbs, clauses, and whole sentences.

Antecedent: The noun that a pronoun doubles for; the antecedent and pronoun must agree in gender, number, and person.

Appositive: A noun or noun phrase that is placed next to another noun or noun phrase to help identify it or to give more specific information.

Article: A type of adjective that tells you whether a noun is definite (*the* bike) or indefinite (*a* bike).

Clause: A group of words that includes a subject and its related verb but that is not necessarily a sentence.

Cliché: A tired, overused phrase.

Collective Noun: A noun that describes a group, such as *team*, *family*, *orchestra*, and *board*.

Comma Splice: A misplaced comma between two main clauses (sentences) that have no conjunction connecting them.

Common Noun: A noun that doesn't refer to any one individual person, place, or thing; a generic name.

Comparative: An adjective or adverb that is used to compare one noun or pronoun to another (e.g., *better, clearer*).

Compound Subject: Two or more subjects connected by a coordinating conjunction.

Conjugation: A fancy word for "working the verb"—verbs change to agree with the subject.

Conjunction: A connector of words, phrases, or parts of sentences.

Contraction: A condensed form of a word or words in which some of the middle letters are missing and often replaced with an apostrophe (e.g., *can't, isn't*).

Coordinate Adjectives: A series of adjectives that describe the same noun; they are separated by commas.

Coordinating Conjunctions: Words that organize sentences or phrases, joining words and phrases of equal importance. See **FANBOYS**.

Correlative Conjunctions: Simple conjunctions that don't function alone; they include *either/or, neither/nor, not only/but also,* and *both/and.*

Cumulative Adjectives: Adjectives that describe the next adjective within a series of adjectives; together they describe the noun; they are not separated by commas.

Dangling Modifier: A word or phrase that describes something that isn't in your sentence.

Definite Article: *The,* which marks a specific or particular noun.

Dependent Clause: A group of words that includes a subject and verb but is incomplete; it depends on something else to complete its thought. Also called subordinate clause.

FANBOYS: The coordinating conjunctions *for, and, nor, but, or, yet,* and *so.*

Fragment: Any phrase or clause that isn't a sentence.

Gerund: A noun made from an action verb + *ing* at the end.

Idiom: An expression that is specific to itself, grammatically speaking; it doesn't follow the rules, and yet it's acceptable the way it is.

Imperative Mood: The verb form used in a commanding sentence (e.g., *Run!*).

Indefinite Article: *A* or *an,* which marks a noun that isn't specific.

Independent Clause: A clause that could be a complete sentence if it stood alone. Also called main clause.

Indicative Mood: The verb form used in a sentence that makes a statement (e.g., *He is home.*).

Infinitive: A form of a verb with the word *to* in front of it (such as *to make*).

Initialism: A type of abbreviation made from the first letter (or letters) of a string of words, not pronounced as a word.

Linking Verb: A verb that expresses a state of being.

Main Clause: See **Independent Clause**.

Modifier: A word or phrase that describes or makes something specific; it can be an adjective or adverb.

Noun: A person, place, or thing.

Object: A person or thing that receives the action of the verb or is the target of a preposition.

Object Pronoun: A pronoun that receives the action of a verb.

Parenthetical Expression: A phrase that is not necessary to the sentence but gives extra information that adds flavor, a sense of style, or an extra thought.

Participial Phrase: A phrase that starts with a participle; it can be at the beginning, middle, or end of a sentence. Also called modifying phrase.

Participle: A verb form that can act as a verb, adjective, or noun; participles of regular verbs end with *ed* or *ing*, and participles of irregular verbs take irregular endings.

Passive Voice: When the action of the verb happens to the subject of a sentence.

Peeve: Something that is particularly annoying, such as a language error; also one of a group of monsters that torment Squiggly and Aardvark.

Phrasal Verb: A set of words (a phrase) that acts as a single verb unit.

Phrases: Groups of words that work together as a grammatical unit in a sentence but are missing something found in a clause such as a subject or a predicate.

Possessive: A noun or pronoun form that indicates ownership, belonging.

Possessive Pronoun: A pronoun that shows ownership.

Predicate: The part of a sentence that contains the verb, and sometimes modifiers, complements, and objects, and says something about the subject.

Predicate Adjective: An adjective that comes after a linking verb and refers to the noun or pronoun before the linking verb.

Preposition: A word that creates a relationship between other words; a preposition often deals with space, time, and direction.

Prepositional Phrase: A group of words that begins with a preposition and ends with a noun or pronoun; it can also contain adjectives, adverbs, articles, etc.

Pronoun: A word that stands in for a noun.

Proper Noun: The name of a specific person, place, or thing.

Qualifier: See **Modifier**.

Reflexive Pronoun: A pronoun that can only be a grammatical object; it's used when the object of the sentence is the same as the subject.

Sentence: A group of words that represent a complete thought; in most cases a sentence will have at least a subject and a verb.

Sentence Adverb: An adverb that describes the whole sentence.

Serial Comma: The last comma before the final conjunction in a list.

Simple Modifier: A one-word modifier or describer (e.g., *only*).

Sir Fragalot: A knight who often speaks in sentence fragments; Grammar Girl's friend.

Split Infinitive: An infinitive with an adverb placed between *to* and the verb (e.g., *to only go*).

Squiggly: A yellow snail; Grammar Girl's friend.

Squinting Modifier: A describer placed between two things, either of which it could be describing, creating confusion for the reader.

Subject: The part of a sentence that defines the person or thing that is expanded on or described by the predicate (e.g., *Bob* ran home).

Subject Pronoun: A pronoun that acts as a subject (e.g., *He* ran home).

Subjunctive Mood: A verb form that communicates feelings, such as wishfulness, hopefulness, or imagination—things that aren't real or true.

Subordinate Clause: Another name for the dependent clause.

Subordinating Conjunctions: Words that join subordinate or dependent clauses to other clauses.

Superlative: A type of adjective or adverb that is used to describe the best or worst of three or more items.

Verb: A word that expresses action or state of being. See also **Action Verb** and **Linking Verb**.

Bibliography

THE FIVE BOOKS I'D RATHER NOT LIVE WITHOUT

The Associated Press Stylebook and Briefing on Media Law. 44th ed. New York: Basic Books, 2009.

Brians, P. *Common Errors in English Usage.* 2nd ed. Wilsonville, Ore.: William, James & Co., 2008.

The Chicago Manual of Style. 15th ed. Chicago: University of Chicago Press, 2003.

Garner, B. *Garner's Modern American Usage.* 3rd ed. New York: Oxford University Press, 2009.

Shaw, H. *Punctuate It Right!* New York: Harper Paperbacks, 1993.

OTHER RESOURCES I USED TO WRITE THIS BOOK

The American Heritage Guide to Contemporary Usage and Style. Boston: Houghton Mifflin Company, 2005.

Burchfield, R. W., ed. *The New Fowler's Modern English Usage.* 3rd ed. New York: Oxford University Press, 1996.

Casagrande, J. *Grammar Snobs Are Great Big Meanies.* New York: Penguin Books, 2006.

Dictionary.com. http://dictionary.reference.com

Hacker, D. *A Writer's Reference.* 6th ed. Boston: Bedford/St. Martin's, 2006.

Lutz, G., and D. Stevenson. *The Writer's Digest Grammar Desk Reference.* Cincinnati: Writer's Digest Books, 2005.

Lynch, J. *Guide to Grammar and style.* http://andromeda.rutgers.edu/~jlynch/Writing

McArthur, T., ed. *Oxford Companion to the English Language.* New York: Oxford University Press, 1992.

Merriam-Webster's Dictionary of English Usage. Springfield, Mass.: Merriam-Webster, 1994.

O'Conner, P. *Woe Is I.* New York: Penguin Putnam, 1996.

Oxford English Dictionary Online. http://www.oed.com

Straus, J. *The Blue Book of Grammar and Punctuation.* 9th ed. Mill Valley, Calif.: Jane Straus, 2006.

Strumpf, M., and A. Douglas. *The Grammar Bible.* New York: Henry Holt and Company, 2004.

Strunk, W., and E. B. White. *The Elements of Style: 50th Anniversary Edition.* New York: Pearson Longman, 2009.

Walsh, B. *Lapsing Into a Comma.* Chicago: Contemporary Books, 2004.

Acknowledgments

Although writing is a solitary practice, no book is written alone. My thanks go to my editor at Henry Holt Books for Young Readers, Sally Doherty, for unflagging patience and encouragement; Laura Godwin for early enthusiasm about the project; Susan Wallach for extensive help with the manuscript; Bonnie Trenga, a frequent guest writer for the Grammar Girl podcast; April Ward for creative design; and the many teachers who have written to me over the years to let me know how much my other books, podcasts, newsletters, and quizzes help them, and who encouraged me to write a book specifically for students.

Finally, language study has a long history, and I owe a debt of gratitude to the many academic linguists, lexicographers, and usage and style guide writers who have come before me. I don't just make this stuff up—without their work, my work wouldn't be possible.

Index

Mignon Fogarty is the creator of *Grammar Girl*™ and the founder and managing director of the *Quick and Dirty Tips*™ network. Formerly a magazine writer, technical writer, and entrepreneur, she has a B.A. in English from the University of Washington in Seattle and an M.S. in biology from Stanford University. She lives in Reno, Nevada. Visit her website at www.quickanddirtytips.com and sign up for the free e-mail grammar tips and podcast.

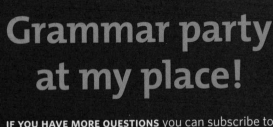

Grammar party at my place!

IF YOU HAVE MORE QUESTIONS you can subscribe to the free weekly Grammar Girl podcast at iTunes, at the Zune Marketplace, or at the Quick and Dirty Tips website (www.quickanddirtytips.com), where you can also subscribe to the free e-mail newsletter I send out every week with a free grammar tip. You can also write (feedback@ quickanddirtytips.com) or call and leave a recorded question (206-338-4475)—you may hear it answered on the show!